ADVICE TO A
YOUNG CRITIC

Bernard Shaw at about the time of writing the
first letters in this volume.

BERNARD SHAW

ADVICE TO A YOUNG CRITIC

Letters 1894-1928

PETER OWEN LIMITED
London

PETER OWEN LIMITED
50 Old Brompton Road
London SW 7

Made and printed in Great Britain by
Boscombe Printing Co. (1933) Ltd., Bournemouth
MCMLVI

Introduction

This new collection of Bernard Shaw letters is not, frankly, all of a piece. Starting definitely as what may well be called "advice to a young critic," the letters changed as the years passed and the interests of both Shaw and Reginald Golding Bright, and the relationship between the two, changed greatly, but the early letters are among the most illuminating concerning Shaw and the history of his early plays that have yet been published. (One pauses parenthetically to lament that there must be literally thousands of letters written by Shaw that have not yet been made public, and the good Shavian shudders at the thought of the hundreds, probably of great interest, that may have been destroyed or never will be made public.)

What is a good Shavian? Since the main interest of the present volume will be for him, it seems worthwhile attempting to define him. I can only paraphrase some words I wrote about five years ago in the course of a review of a book of Shavian biography and criticism. Shortly before his death on November 1st, 1950, Shaw, in a preface to fellow-Fabian G. D. H. Cole's volume of selections from Samuel Butler, stated that Darwin was no more a Darwinist than he himself was a Shavian. Like most of his pronouncements, this was multiple-barrelled. But among other things Shaw surely meant that in his mid-nineties he was not an academic researcher amid the vast and still constantly increasing library of comment and criticism, of debate and diatribe, of biography and bunk, written about himself. In that sense Shaw was not a Shavian. Refusing a year before his death to read a review of his neighbour Winsten's confused and confusing book about him and of his own *Sixteen Self Sketches* sent to him by one of my editors, G.B.S. explained: "The Shavian Essayists are often not only good friends and faithful fans, but interesting authors on their own account. But they should be read for their own sakes, not for mine." In the sense that I am myself a Shavian, I would define the term as meaning one who is still a good friend to Shaw (although not necessarily one actually acquainted during his lifetime), a faithful fan, and an avid reader of the works of the Shavian Essayists. And one must insist that not all of the latter have been good Shavians (with critical integrity necessary to him who has closely studied the critical tenets and the critical credo of the Master himself, one must deny the title, for instance, to G. K. Chesterton, Archibald Henderson, Frank Harris, Stephen Winsten, and Louis Kronenberger). Wherefore this new volume of intimate personal revelation becomes the more valuable. And if it would seem that I am defending myself, I assert that, while it is not the necessary business of an editor to be an "interesting author," nothing is lost in this instance by his being a good Shavian.

The present volume lacks the combined graces of style, of personal emotional appeal and of give-and-take of the correspondence with the inimitable Ellen Terry and the unpredictable Mrs. Pat Campbell, but the early letters as a group and many of the later ones are written in Shaw's best vein, if not in his most perfect style ; they provide much additional evidence of some of his finer qualities and characteristics ; and they either offer really new information or firmly settle hitherto moot points concerning his career and his works.

The first and the third letters, for instance, sound out conclusively Shaw's steady critical credo, already by 1894 well thought out during years of reviewing of musical performances, and to be religiously followed and developed during his years as dramatic critic : integrity and fair-mindedness combined, security of the critical self, respect for the performer or performing organisation criticised. The third, dated December 2, 1894, with the accompanying manuscript of Bright, is probably unique as an example of meticulously careful and purely gratuitous and altruistic editing of the work of a beginner by a truly established critic of the arts, if as yet an untried fully-fledged dramatic critic. It is one of the most important examples of pure statement and of pure style that I have encountered, even in Shaw's own words.

The fourth entry, dated December 14th, 1894, is, like so many letters in this new collection, equally notable for pointed practical advice and for illuminating self-revelation. As Shaw tirelessly repeated during his active writing life (the first letter was written during his thirty-eighth year and he died in his ninety-fifth), he was always generous with autobiographical details, but even to the tireless Shavian researcher this volume presents new, necessary, and indispensable Shavian material.

For example, if the ever-generous and reliably charitable Shaw had any real *bêtes noires* during his long critical career, surely they were the fictional Paula Tanqueray of Sir Arthur Wing Pinero and the indubitably real and English Brodribb who was to become, shortly after this correspondence began, and partly, one more than suspects, at the instance of a well-known critic famous as G.B.S., Sir Henry Irving. The letter of April 22nd, 1895, attempting to argue young Bright out of his worship of his "Dulcinea," Paula Tanqueray, and the self-interview, dated May 15th, 1897, concerning the much-debated matter of Irving's refusal to produce Shaw's "The Man of Destiny," therefore, would by themselves make this volume invaluable to all future students of late nineteenth-century dramatic and theatrical history and criticism.

II

If the true Shavian be, as I have posited, an indefatigable reader of all that concerned Shaw in any way, it will be obvious that I reacted with enormous interest and equal impatience some two years ago to the announcement of two publications, one English, the correspondence of Bernard Shaw with R. Golding Bright, and one American, Bernard Shaw, *Advice to a Young Critic*. It was, therefore, with something more than approaching real alarm that I discovered myself three months ago embarked upon the editing of both volumes, which turned out to be identical. Let me express my gratitude to the following for help in finishing the task : the great critic, John Gassner ; Eric J. Batson, secretary of The Shaw Society of London, who laboured under pressure in London to do the work there that I should myself have undertaken ; George Freedley, Curator of the Theatre Collection of the New York Public Library ; and various of my colleagues here in the foothills of the Rockies who uncomplainingly answered—usually over the telephone— numerous and usually unexplained strange questions. I suppose some credit also must be given to one of the most inexplicable inventions of the modern world, the researching mind, that accumulator of unconsidered, if not eventually inconsiderable, scraps of information, trifles so handy in annotating at top- speed and in the midst of the pressure of the graduate-degree mill such a volume as this.

To my scholarly disconcertion, my most difficult task was discovering something about the man to whom Shaw wrote these letters. For, as I have noted, and as I would re-emphasise, this volume presents a one-sided correspondence. One manuscript (printed ? who knows ? not I) and several printed notices of R. E. Golding Bright are included, as are several business notes from Shaw to Elizabeth Marbury, American play-agent whose London office Bright managed after the death of his elder brother, and to Ada Wooldridge, secretary in that office. (The correspondence was selected and put together from the files of Golding Bright by Miss Joan Ling, herself now a London play- agent.) Apparently either Bright did not bother to save, or his executrix to copy, his own side of the correspondence, and it is distinctly obvious that with Shaw's overwhelming correspondence, *he* could not afford to keep Bright's letters. As a note to the first entry suggests, not even that amazingly assiduous biographer Hesketh Pearson seems to have been aware of this correspondence, and Eric Batson has written me that many informed Londoners " did not realise that G.B. *had* been Shaw's agent for so long ! " Aside from one reference to him by Pearson, noted in my first separate commentary, Bright has never been mentioned by name in a work on Shaw, although, as I point out later, Shaw himself did, in a letter to Ellen Terry dated May 13th, 1897, anonymously mention " a young journalist in whom I am interested " to whom he had given the dialogue of the interview with Irving concerning " The Man of Destiny." Until the publication of the present volume, that reference has meant nothing to Shavian students.

The father of Golding Bright was a doctor, as had been many of his ancestors (one, Dr. Richard Bright, having in 1827 identified and named Bright's disease), residing at 153 Sunderland Road, Forest Hill, London, S.E. Golding, born some time in 1874 before April 14th, was working in an office in the City when he first wrote to Shaw. The reader of these letters will note Shaw's sympathy with young Bright's desire to get out of the office, he himself having been a clerk, and a very successful one, in a Dublin estate agent's office in the early 'seventies. Bright's father obviously did not approve of his ambition to become a dramatic critic, possibly because an older brother, Arthur Addison, had already become both a journalist and, at least as early as 1891, an actor's agent and play broker. The course of Golding Bright's career up to the beginning of 1928 is made clear in the following letters or in the annotations. When Elisabeth Marbury died in 1933, he went on with his work as London representative of The American Play Company and was working in the same capacity for the Richard J. Madden Play Company at the time of his death.

My London correspondent reported that Bright was "publicity-shy" (I later hazard the conjecture that this may have been the result not only of temperament but also of reaction to Addison's suicide on May 29th, 1906), and my London correspondent was not able to find out much about Bright in London. It is evident, however, that in his later years he was a well-known figure at London first-nights, one of distinction and dignity, with silvery short hair and a charming smile, always sitting in the same stall, always in immaculate evening dress, with the swinging black cape, top hat, white gloves, and gold-headed cane of a bygone era. Eric Batson informs me that, according to London gossip, at these first-nights he "often went to sleep!" So, for that matter, did Shaw's great friend, that respected critic, William Archer, so often to be referred to in this volume. But Mr. Batson goes on to record of Bright that, unlike Archer: "When he awoke he would forecast pretty exactly how long the play would run." Viola Meynell, in her edition of *Letters of J. M. Barrie* (1947), included four and a half pages of letters from Barrie to Bright, dealing mainly with matters of the filming of the Scot's plays. Arnold Bennett referred to Bright in passing three times in his *Journals*, twice as agent, once as husband of "George Egerton." Lady Cynthia Asquith, in her recent *Portrait of Barrie*, recorded that all matters concerning production of the plays, while she was Barrie's secretary, were referred to his "trusted agent," Golding Bright. Barrie, as we shall see later, had remained to the very end the loyal friend of the older brother, Addison. Elisabeth Marbury, in her reminiscences, *My Crystal Ball* (1923), noted her sense of "extreme good fortune" in persuading Golding to assume Addison's position, on the latter's death, as her London representative, and spoke of him admiringly if briefly: "He keeps ahead of his time. He was born a modern. His judgment as to the merit of a manuscript is rarely at fault."

The little that I have been able to find out about Golding

Bright, recorded in the notes or summarised above, accords with an appreciation of him by the late Valentine Williams, published in the London *Times* ten days after his death. It suggests in maturity a personality but faintly shadowed forth by the brash young man who forced himself upon the attention of Shaw on the night of April 21st, 1894, and who wrote to him soon thereafter for the first time. One laments in reading this tribute from a friend, as frequently when reading Shaw's letters to him, that " My dear G.B." 's side of the correspondence is not also available. For one gathers there was in the brash youth of twenty something which suggested to the intuitive Shaw the charm of personality of the man who died at sixty-seven, and of whom. Williams in the London *Times* of April 24th, 1941, wrote :

With the death on Easter Monday after a long illness of Golding Bright the theatre in England and America has lost one of its best-known and most influential figures. For many years London's leading play agent, his notable list of clients included J. M. Barrie, Bernard Shaw, and Somerset Maugham. But Golding Bright was a great deal more than a shrewd and capable dramatic critic with an unrivalled knowledge of the theatre in all its aspects, who looked after his clients' interests with unremitting zeal. His judgment of a play was rarely at fault, and his great experience was frequently called upon by playwrights and managers alike in the difficult period that lies between the writing of a play and its presentation in the theatre. Many well-known actors and actresses owe their careers to his flair for casting. He was a familiar figure at London first-nights, and " Golding " in his stall will be greatly missed. The deep sympathy of his host of friends will go out to his wife, the distinguished writer " George Egerton," his devoted companion during 40 years of married life, who nursed him at his express wish during his last illness.

Were the mere editor of a volume of letters permitted a dedication, mine would be to the author of these letters, and for the inscription I would repeat some words I wrote to Eric

11

Batson a couple of years ago : "Alive he haunted me. Dead he seems more alive than ever." After living intensively and intensely with these letters for a bare three months, I would repeat these words with greater and more passionate sincerity. I have loved the man for some forty years, just this side of idolatry. The editing of this volume—however inadequately carried out, and I think I realise its shortcomings better than any other man will—has been a labour of love in the ultimate sense. I beg from Shaw's reverend shade and from his still living and breathing personality pardon for any sins of commission or omission. What sins there be, venial or mortal, they are mine alone. *Mea apologia?* No. *Mea culpa.*

E. J. WEST.

Boulder, Colorado.
September 5th, 1955.

Private.   29 Fitzroy Square, W.

                                              30th April, 1894.

Dear Sir,

Your letter has only just reached me. They did not forward
it from the theatre, expecting a visit from me every day.

There is no way of becoming a dramatic critic. It happens
by accident. For instance, I have never been offered a post of
the kind, though I should have been quite willing to take it any
time these last eighteen years. But when the accident happens,
it happens to a journalist. It is to men who are already in the
profession, and known as men who can write and who know
the ways of papers, that editors turn when a vacancy occurs.
If you work for a paper as a reporter or paragraphist, and are
keen on theatres, you can generally do a stray notice on an
emergency which makes you known to the editor as having a
turn that way. Then, if the dramatic critic dies, or goes to
another paper, or drops journalism, you have your chance of
succeeding him, if you have shown the requisite capacity. That
is the regular way. But you may induce some friend who starts
a paper, or becomes editor of one, to give you a trial straight
off ; but that is a matter of pure luck, with, of course, the skill
to take the luck when it comes. Remember, to be a critic, you
must be not only a bit of an expert in your subject, but you
must also have literary skill, and trained critical skill, too—the
power of analysis, comparison, etc. I have had to go through
years of work as a reviewer of books, a critic of pictures, a
writer on political and social questions, and a musical critic, in
order to qualify myself for the post I now hold on the staff of
The World. You must not think that because you only heard
of me for the first time the other day or thereabouts that I got
such reputation as I have cheaply. I came to London in 1876,
and have been fighting for existence ever since. Even my little

platform performance at the Playgoers' Club was the result of about fifteen years' practice of public speaking, mostly under the humblest circumstances. I tell you this lest you should be discouraged and embittered by thinking that you are meeting with exceptional and unfair difficulties. In London all beginners are forty, with twenty years of obscure hard work behind them ; and, believe me, those obscure twenty years are not the worst part of one's life, nor need you nor anyone be afraid to face them.

I still hold to it that a man who thinks a dramatic performance worth waiting at the pit door all day for is a lunatic. The front row of the pit is worth something ; but it is not worth that. However, I only give you my own valuation. If your enthusiasm makes it worth the trouble to you, I have no right to object.

All the views which you attribute to me concerning Mr. Irving and W. Tree and the " new school " have, if you will excuse my saying so, been put into your mind by newspaper paragraphs written by people who have not the slightest knowledge of me or my views. There is nothing that annoys me more than all this nonsense about new schools and the new drama and the rest of it. I suffer from it considerably, as it leads people to construe purely dramatic passages in my plays as interpolations of what are supposed to be my political views. But even if the play did contain any such interpolation, I should not admit your right to make a disturbance on the head of it. If the Fabians in the gallery were enjoying my play, as I am glad to say that the gallery still does now that there are no longer any Fabians in it, why did you carry your disapproval of a purely imaginary allusion to the Royal Family to the point of making them lose patience with you ? Have they ever disturbed you in the enjoyment of the patriotic and loyal sentiments with which popular military melodramas are freely spiced ? We have both been present, I have no doubt, at first nights of plays containing a good deal that is exceedingly repugnant to my political and moral opinions. I don't think you have ever found me inter-rupting an actor or annoying my neighbour on that account. I simply do not go to the sort of plays I dislike.

In conclusion, let me assure you that I did my best to put before you a true picture of what a brave soldier who knows his business really is. I heartily wish you could bring me an audience of veterans—of men who know what it is to ride a bolting horse in a charge, or to trust to the commissariat for food during a battle, or to be under fire for two or three days : they would not have taken my chocolate, etc., etc., for silly jokes, as I feel a good many of the audience did.

Yours faithfully,

G. Bernard Shaw.

29 Fitzroy Square, W.

19th November, 1894.

Dear Sir,

Your letter surprised me, because, as it happened, I had just sent your name to an editor who wanted a dramatic critic ; and it seemed odd that we should think of one another simul-taneously. However, as the position in question—that of the criticship of *The Saturday Review* under Frank Harris—was one which could only as a very bold experiment have been given

15

to a comparatively untried hand, Harris was probably more disposed to damn my eyes for refusing the berth myself than to entertain my suggestion of an alternative.

By all means make *The Sun* pay you. But if you can afford it, let the account run until it is large enough to save the appearance of worrying about a trifle—say until it is over a couple of pounds or so. Never allow a regular commercial newspaper to get copy from you for nothing ; but never, either, if you can afford it, shew any anxiety about being paid. Take it as a matter of course that what is worth publishing is worth paying for.

The title " Mrs. Jarman's Profession " is a curious illustration of the influence of Paula Tanqueray. The real title is " Mrs. Warren's Profession." The name Jarman never came into my head, nor is there any authority for it except some association of ideas in Grem's head which led him to give the wrong name to his interviewer.

My separation from *The World* is permanent. I made up my mind to take the opportunity of Edmund Yates's death to escape from musical criticism, which is not so amusing to the writer who has written a long article on the subject every week for seven years as it is to his readers. I have an article on musical criticism in a forthcoming number of *The Scottish Musical Monthly*. I will ask the editor to send you a copy.

My successor, Mr. Hitchens (or whatever his name is), seems to me to write cleverly and pleasantly enough. You must give up detesting everything appertaining to Oscar Wilde or to anyone else. The critic's first duty is to admit, with absolute respect, the right of every man to his own style. Wilde's wit and his fine literary workmanship are points of great value. There is always a vulgar cry both for and against every man or woman of any distinction ; and from such cries you cannot keep your mind too clear if you wish to attain distinction yourself. You know the sort of thing I mean : you have heard it about Whistler, Sarah Grand, Ibsen, Wagner—everybody who has a touch of genius.

16

Excuse this scrap of sermon : I would not intrude it upon you if I did not know by experience the great difficulty of forming and holding to a genuine original opinion of public men on their own merits when so many fools are chattering about them in all directions.

Keep up your courage : from what you tell me you are getting on very well as far as the papers are concerned. But you ought to write a couple of books on the drama. Burn them afterwards by all means ; but write them. I started by writing five books, one after the other, without producing the least impression on an apparently implacable destiny.

I am overwhelmed with work in connection with the School-board and Vestry elections and have only time to send this hastiest of scrawls.

Yours faithfully,

G. Bernard Shaw.

Private.   29 Fitzroy Square, W.

2nd December, 1894.

Dear Sir,

The best service I can do you is to take your notice and jot down on it without ceremony the comments which occur to me. You will find first certain alterations in black ink. In them I have tried to say, as well as I can off-hand, what you were trying to say : that is, since it was evident you were dodging round some point or other, I have considered the only point that there was to make, and have made it. It came quite easy when I had altered your statement about Frenchmen at large to what you really meant—the conventional stage Frenchman. Always find out rigidly and exactly what you mean, and never strike an attitude, whether national or moral or critical or anything else. You struck a national attitude when you wrote that about the Frenchman and Englishman ; and you struck a moral attitude when you wrote " She has sunk low enough in all conscience." Get your facts right first : that is the foundation of all style, because style is the expression of yourself ; and you cannot express yourself genuinely except on a basis of precise reality.

In red ink you will find some criticisms which you may confidently take as expressing what an experienced editor would think of your sample of work.

You have not at all taken in my recommendation to you to write a book. You say you are scarcely competent to write books just yet. That is just why I recommend you to learn. If I advised you to learn to skate, you would not reply that your balance was scarcely good enough yet. A man learns to skate by staggering about and making a fool of himself. Indeed, he progresses in all things by resolutely making a fool of himself. You will never write a good book until you have written some bad ones. If they have sent you my Scottish article, you will see that I began by writing some abominably bad criticisms. I wrote five long books before I started again on press work. William Archer wrote a long magnum opus on the life and works of Richard Wagner, a huge novel, and a book on the drama, besides an essay on Irving and a good deal of leader work for a Scotch paper, before he began his victorious career on *The World*. He also perpetrated about four plays in his early days. (By the way, you mustn't publish this information.) You must go through the mill, too ; and you can't possibly start too soon. Write a thousand words a day for the next five years for at least nine

months every year. Read all the great critics—Ruskin, Richard
Wagner, Lessing, Lamb and Hazlitt. Get a ticket for the British
Museum reading room, and live there as much as you can. Go
to all the first-rate orchestral concerts and to the opera, as well
as to the theatres. Join debating societies and learn to speak in
public. Haunt little Sunday evening political meetings and
exercise that accomplishment. Study men and politics in this
way. As long as you stay in the office, try and be the smartest
hand in it : I spent four and a half years in an office before I
was twenty. Be a teetotaller ; don't gamble ; don't lend ; don't
borrow ; don't for your life get married ; make the attainment
of EFFICIENCY your sole object for the next fifteen years ;
and if the City can teach you nothing more, or demands more
time than you can spare from your apprenticeship, tell your
father that you prefer to cut loose and starve, and *do it*. But it
will take you at least a year or two of tough work before you
will be able to build up for yourself either the courage or the
right to take heroic measures. Finally, since I have given you
all this advice, I add this crowning precept, the most valuable
of all. NEVER TAKE ANYBODY'S ADVICE.

And now, to abandon the rôle of your guide, philosopher
and friend, which I don't propose to revert to again until you
report progress in ten years or so, let me thank you for the
paragraph in *The Sun*, which was quite right and appropriate.
I have no more news at present, except that I have nearly finished
a new play, the leading part in which I hope to see played by
Miss Janet Achurch, of whose genius I have always had a very
high opinion. It is quite a sentimental play, which I hope to
find understood by women, if not by men ; and it is so straightforward that I expect to find it pronounced a miracle of
perversity. This is my fifth dramatic composition. The first was
" Widowers' Houses," of Independent Theatre fame. The second
was " The Philanderer," a topical comedy in which the New
Woman figured before Mr. Grundy discovered her. The third

was "Mrs. Warren's Profession," a play with a purpose, the purpose being much the same as that of my celebrated letter to the *Pall Mall Gazette* on the Empire controversy. The fourth was "Arms and the Man," which was so completely misunderstood that it made my reputation as a playwright both here and in New York. The Independent Theatre has already announced "Mrs. Warren's Profession" for its forthcoming season. "The Philanderer" was written originally for that society; but on its completion I threw it aside and wrote another more suitable for the purposes of the society—Mrs. Warren. Wyndham asked me to do something for him on seeing "Arms and the Man"; and I tried to persuade him to play "The Philanderer; but whilst the project was under consideration, Wyndham made such a decisive success with "Rebellious Susan" that he resolved to follow up the vein of comedy opened by Henry Arthur Jones to the end before venturing upon the Shavian quicksand. But this involved so long a delay that I withdrew the play, and am now looking round to see whether the world contains another actor who can philander as well as Wyndham. As I have always said that if I did not write six plays before I was forty I would never write one after, I must finish the work now in hand and another as well before the 26th July, 1896; but I hope to do much more than that, since I have managed to get through the present play within three months, during which I have had to take an active part in the Schoolboard and Vestry elections, to keep up my work in the Fabian Society, to deliver nearly two dozen lectures in London and the provinces, and to fire off various articles and criticisms. The fact is, I took a good holiday this autumn in Germany, Italy, and in Surrey; and I accumulated a stock of health which I am dissipating at a frightful rate. The Christmas holidays will come just in time to save my life.

If any of this stuff is of use to you for paragraphing purposes —and remember that the world will not stand too much Bernard Shaw—you are welcome to work it up by all means when it suits you. Only, don't quote it as having been said by me. That is an easy way out which I bar.

I find that you have got an atrociously long letter out of me. I have been blazing away on the platform this evening for an hour and a half, and ought to be in bed instead of clattering at this machine.

Yours, half asleep,

G. Bernard Shaw.

R. Golding Bright, Esq.,

Playgoers' Club.

"ODETTE" AT THE PRINCESS'S

When a stage hero discovers firstly a Russian Prince creeping about his drawing-room at midnight, and secondly, his wife in undress standing at her bedroom door, whispering her lover's name, what course shall he pursue? If a Frenchman, he must kill his wife and fight her seducer. If an Englishman he is permitted to seek redress in the Divorce Court. Lord Henry Trevene, being in the impossible position of a French stage hero translated into English, finds both these plain paths of duty barred to him. Accordingly, he denies the justice of a law which unties the nuptial knot only as a preliminary to uniting the guilty lovers. He can see full well what his own future will be—a hopeless blank. So be it! But Odette's life shall be no better. His wife she shall remain till the end, though he will no longer

21

tolerate her presence under the same roof. Go she must and that very night, whilst he will retain their only child, an infant daughter.

Fifteen years elapse, the child Eva has developed into a charming girl of eighteen summers, who knows nothing of the past, but has been taught to believe her mother dead. Eva is engaged to Lord Shandon, and the only bar to their mutual happiness is his mother's sanction, which can be gained by a promise from Odette never to call herself by her married name again, and never to set foot either in Paris or London. At Nice, where all the parties are stopping, Lord Henry sends an ambassador in the person of Philip Eden to induce his wife to consent to these terms. She has sunk low enough in all conscience, living in an establishment that is neither more nor less than a gambling hell kept by an American quack doctor, who never *loses* at cards. In debt, in difficulties, she none the less refuses the proposal of an increased allowance on such conditions. " Sweet is revenge, especially to women." It's her turn now, and she means to make the most of it ; she demands to see her child for whom her maternal instinct, though dormant, is yet alive. To this proposition Lord Henry very weakly consents, provided that she does not reveal her identity. The interview between mother and daughter takes place, when Odette strives to awaken her child's memory to herself, and failing, leaves husband and child alone once more.

Mr. Clement Scott has been pleased to designate this a problem play, thereby seeking to prove that long before " The Second Mrs. Tanqueray " was produced, London had dealt with the subject. But then every play that touches real life at all is a problem play. The only question that interests us is whether it is a " solution-of-the-problem " play. And will anyone seriously contend that the course taken by Lord Henry is a solution of the problem of how to deal with an unfaithful wife ? The famous ' Tue-la ' of Dumas fils is reasonable in comparison, and our own divorce court appears a quite divinely wise institution beside the silliness of Lord Henry. [Shaw's comment : ' Here, having disposed of the problem business, you must start a new paragraph, criticising the play *as a play* solely.'] It appears to me that Sardou blundered not once but many times in the construction of his play. [Shaw's comment : 'And you mustn't tell a man like Sardou that it appears to you that he has blundered : you must point out what you object to and why you object to it.'] It may be that, as it was written some fifteen years ago, and produced in England under the Bancroft régime in '82, it appears stilted and old-fashioned in thought and idea ; but under no circumstances can it be called a great play. [Underlining here by Shaw. His comment : ' It does not pretend to be a great play. The remark is equally true of Box & Cox, which is nevertheless a very good farce. The question is, is Odette a good play *of its class,* and what you mean is that it isn't.'] One feels instinctively that Sardou has got ' no forrader,' whereas Mr. Pinero with " The Second Mrs. Tanqueray " really handles a dangerous theme most delicately and infuses a strain of genius into his work. [Foregoing underlined passage crossed out by Shaw. His comment : ' You must make an oath never to mention Mrs. Tanqueray again, or even think of her. The one chief and damning disability of the young critic is that he always has some pet author and pet work for whose supremacy he is mortally *jealous.* He becomes a knight-errant indicating the superiority of his Dulcinea over all other ladies. Mrs. Tanqueray is your Dulcinea ; and you will never be worth a guinea a column until you grow out of her.']

When Mrs. Anna Ruppert made her début as Camille some four months since, she won the good opinion of Mr. Clement Scott, who informed his readers that the lady possessed every quality needed for a successful stage-career. I do not for one moment wish to set myself up—[Foregoing underlined passage crossed out by Shaw. His comment : ' Yes, you *do* wish to set

yourself up, and you are going on to do it in the next line. Why
shouldn't you ? Why deliberately say what you don't mean ?]—
against so distinguished a critic, but I am quite unable to side
with him on this point. " I must be cruel only to be kind."
[Foregoing underlined passage crossed out by Shaw. His comment : ' *Never* say a thing like this. There is nothing more
offensive to artists—and rightly so—than to make a show of
sparing their feelings. It is right to be considerate, but horribly
wrong to show it.'] Au contraire—[Obliterated by Shaw. His
comment : ' This unnecessary and self-conscious exculpation is
awful. The public is supposed to understand a critic's position
without being told ')—I admire her pluck in attempting to make
a success out of a play which, with the alluring personality of
Modjeska, failed to attract. But Mrs. Ruppert is unfortunately
not an actress at all. Her performance was amateurish to a fault.
She has not learned the first principles of elocution or acting
—[Crossed out by Shaw. His comment : ' You *musn't* talk about
first principles : they don't exist. Poor Mrs. R. had been drilled
to within an inch of her life in " the principles " of elocution ']—
nor can she even tread the stage with dignity. Her voice is hard,
unsympathetic and monotonous—[Shaw's comment : ' Now we
are coming to something sensible. You are quite entitled to
describe her voice : that is quite a different thing to talking about
" the principles of elocution and acting " ']—and her pathos is
deliciously comic. She no more realised the light and shade of
Odette's nature than would a schoolgirl appreciate the hidden
beauty and poetry of Ophelia or the sublime tragedy of Mrs.
Tanqueray. [Crossed out by Shaw. His comment : ' No,
Reginald, no. Not again.'] In taking to the stage, Mrs. Ruppert
has clearly mistaken her vocation, and the sooner she realises
this fact the better it will be for her pocket. [Foregoing crossed
out by Shaw. His comment : ' It is no part of a dramatic critic's
business to make such a remark, which would have been equally
true of a fine actress playing the best sort of dramatic poetry.']

If the leading lady be weak, however, the rest of the company certainly are not. One piece of acting stands out <u>most</u> vividly, and may possibly drag the play into the quiet waters of success. The audience, annoyed by the incompetence of the manageress, readily appreciated Mr. Charles Warner's skilful impersonation of Lord Henry. We have been too apt to regard this actor as a breezy hero of melodrama only, but last night Mr. Warner proved how mistaken we all were, by playing this trying and difficult part, which is almost wholly in one key, to <u>perfection</u>. [Underlined by Shaw. His comment: 'Rather strong, eh? It leaves no room for Salvini, or Irving.'] <u>Undoubtedly</u>—[Crossed out by Shaw. His comment: ' " Undoubtedly " is not the right way to put it. Many other critics doubted it and ridiculed it. You mean that it *seemed to you* one of the finest, &c., &c.']— it is one of the very finest things he has ever done, worthy of a place next his hauntingly terrible Conpean. Here and there, per- chance, one could detect a false note, a misplaced emphasis ; but the whole was so excellent, and <u>played with so firm a grip and manly (never degenerating to maudlin) pathos, that such slight excrescences may</u> readily be condoned. [Underlining by Shaw. His comment: 'Now here you are saying something definite—you are writing criticism—you are *describing* what you saw. Don't you feel how much better it is than mere pompous and unmeaning phrase-slinging like " Undoubtedly it is one of the finest things he has done, &c." ? '] Scarcely less deserving of praise was the cynic Johnny Stratford, sustained with rare skill—[Shaw's comment : ' This is all right—quite presentable '] —and a keen eye for artistic effect by Mr. Bernard Gould. Quite adequate, too, were Miss Ettie Williams as the *ingénue,* and Mr. Herbert Flemming as Philip Eden. If only Mrs. Ruppert the manageress will induce Mrs. Ruppert the would-be actress to retire in favour of someone else more fitted for the part, there might perhaps be a long lease of life in store for this so-called ' problem ' play.   R. E. G. B.

29 Fitzroy Square, **W.**

14th December, 1894.

Dear Sir,

The paragraph does not refer to " Mrs. Warren's Profession," which has not yet been submitted to the Censor. I do not know what it refers to. It sounds like Henry James and Alexander ; but I have heard nothing about it.

This year license was refused by Mr. Pigott to a play by Mr. Sydney Olivier, who, as an upper division clerk in the Colonial Office, ranks as a more highly qualified man than Mr. Pigott, whose appointment is a matter of patronage, and who might quite possibly be an illiterate person, whereas an upper division civil servant has to pass a very stiff examination. The licence was applied for by Miss Farr, who wished to produce the play at the Avenue Theatre. Mr. Olivier attempted to discuss the question with Mr. Pigott, but found him to be an ignorant and prejudiced opponent of the movement begun by Ibsen. It was quite useless to talk to him : he was well-intentioned enough, but incapable. This is the only recent example of Censorial despotism with which I am acquainted.

Do not write a book with the purpose of burning it. Write it on the assumption that it is going to be published and to be useful and successful. Then see what will happen. Probably you will be unable to find a publisher ; and you will have learnt so much by the effort of writing it that you will go on afresh and pass it by. But don't burn it, even if you become ashamed of it. Keep it in a drawer somewhere. At thirty, you will be impatient of the stuff you wrote at twenty ; but at forty, you will recover some of your respect for the dreams of your youth. Besides, it may turn out worth publishing. One never knows. The one certain thing is you must write, write, write every day for several years if you are to become a master workman in your profession.

As to your suggestion that perhaps I was better able to afford such exercises than you, I can only say that the difference between us appears to be that your father is fairly well off, whereas mine was poor and embarrassed. If your board and lodging are guaranteed, you may consider yourself a king. If you had seen me about twelve years ago, you would have seen a grimly shabby figure. For about nine years after I came to London I made nothing and wrote a good deal. Then for five or six years I made about £150. Then for a few years I made nearly £300. At present my income has gone back to its old figure—0. So you see money does not matter so much. A prosperous stockbroker would consider my career a dismal one ; but, as a matter of fact, if you consider the variety of my interests and activities, the friends I have made (not to mention the enemies), the consideration I enjoy, and the degree of personal efficiency I have acquired, you will, I think, see that if I had devoted myself to making several thousand a year as a stockbroker, I should have made a very bad bargain. And remember that I began as much handicapped by poverty, shyness, awkwardness, and all the miseries of weak immaturity as anybody could have done. You have probably twice my opportunities and advantages, if not ten times. The fact is that everybody has to stand the same racket more or less—more if he is penniless, less if he has a father who guarantees a roof and a meal. So go ahead : the world's your oyster.

G. B. S.

29 Fitzroy Square, **W.**

11th January, 1895.

Dear Sir,

The worst of this paragraphing business is that it deals so much with persons and brings you across all manner of personal dislikes and quarrels which cause your work to be thrown aside through no fault of your own. For instance, Runciman, the musical critic of *The Saturday,* who is perhaps the best of recent editorial finds in the way of a critic, was for a time writing for *The Sun.* They actually dismissed him out of sheer inability to know a good man when they had got hold of one. Being a good man, he has character enough to make enemies. So has Frank Harris. So have I. A paragraph about all three of us has several chances against it in any newspaper office in London. As you probably saw, I ran the gauntlet in *The Star* successfully, though I do not know who the paragraphist was. I think you would do well to invest a few shillings (only three, I think) in a huge volume called Sell's Dictionary of the World's Press, Fleet Street, near Fetter Lane, and study it carefully with a view to seeing what you could do in the way of manifolding your paragraphs and sending them simultaneously to several papers throughout the country. I have not had experience enough of this sort of journalism to advise you as to details ; but it seems to me that this is a thing that an enterprising man ought to do. If you could persuade your father to equip you with a Remington or North typewriter (these are the best for such rough handling as manifolding requires) as part of the necessary outfit of a young man desirous of being up-to-date in an office, you could make at least ten copies of a paragraph with carbon paper, and send them simultaneously to ten different papers in ten different districts, with, of course, a chance of two or three of them being

28

inserted. You could offer a weekly column of theatrical gossip and news at a low price—say ten or fifteen shillings—to a number of papers whose circulations do not overlap, and whose day of publication is the same, and try to make it pay by getting more than one paper to take it. But be careful to see that the proprietors of the papers you approach are different, as there are some provincial newspapers which are practically duplicates issued by the same firm in widely distant parts of the kingdom. Even if you don't succeed, you will pick up a certain knowledge of the press, and you will find out the sort of questions you ought to put to the men who do make this sort of thing pay. It is always worth while to do a thing the wrong way in order to find out how not to do it, which is an important step towards finding out how to do it.

I am much obliged to you for your appreciation of my *Saturday* articles. In a way, your opinion of Grundy's play is fairer than mine, as you take the thing on its merits, whereas I am partly fighting against the leading of the drama further in a direction which I believe to be, for the present, the wrong direction. And I greatly dislike the clumsy device (as it seems to me) of " the reasoner " introduced to explain the play—the Thouvenin of Dumas *fils*. The courage that struck you as to the ending was discounted for me by two things. First, the wretched claptrap about " the thin red line," which, as you may imagine, did not seem very courageous to the author of "Arms and the Man " ; and second, the stupidity of the conclusion that there is no solution of the difficulty of unhappy marriages, whereas there is a perfectly simple solution in reform of the divorce laws. In some American States, South Dakota for instance, those four people could have re-sorted themselves quite easily. It is quite a feature of stageland and the aloofness of our theatrical people from real life that dramatists are always propounding as Sphinx-enigma questions that every practical man knows the answer to, whilst they skip light-heartedly over situations which in real life raise the most appalling difficulties. As to the acting, poor Brandon Thomas, of course, did what he could, and did it very well, to pull off an impossible part. I saw the play in the second night ; and Miss Calhoun, though not bad as far as she went, certainly did not do as much as she might have done with that one scene which was all that justified the existence of the play, and was, in fact, the root of it. You must not dismiss Gilbert Hare as beneath contempt. Suppose your father bought *The World,* and handed over the theatrical column to you, you would at first probably disappoint the readers who were accustomed to Archer's work. But if you turned out a fairly presentable column, and really did your blood best, correcting every sentence carefully and taking your work earnestly, all the good men who had been through the mill would admit that you had a right to your trial. If you want to enjoy masterly acting twenty years hence, you must be very tender to the apprentices and journeymen of today.

I doubt if I shall republish my *Saturday* articles. I never could be persuaded to do so with my *World* articles. Taken out of the atmosphere of the week in which they were written, they lost half their freshness.

G. B. S.

29 Fitzroy Square, W.

30th January, 1895.

Dear Mr. Bright,

This is just the sort of case in which children are atrociously cruel to their parents. The first thing to do is to clear your mind of all protests against the position of your father's wife. No matter who or what she is or was, or whether you and your brothers and sisters like or dislike her, your father's claim to be happy with the woman he prefers and to marry her, and put her interests before those of everyone else, is indisputable. Of course, it is a very disagreeable turn of events for the family, but it is not a grievance. If you take it in bad part, you will do pure, unmitigated, useless harm, since the marriage cannot be undone (even if it were reasonable to demand that it should) ; and besides, by making your father's relation with his children resentful and miserable, you will throw him more helplessly than ever on the sympathy of his wife, and almost drive him to make an unfair division of his property in her favour when he dies.

Fifty pounds a year is a fortune to a man in your position. You can't take hansoms on it, nor patronise the three-and-sixpenny lunch and the seven-and-sixpenny *table d'hote* at the Criterion on it, nor go to the stalls on it, nor live in a Whitehall Court flat on it ; but you can keep yourself on it much better than most City clerks can keep a wife and family on it. With such an endowment you haven't the ghost of a claim on your father, though you must bid a long farewell to the style of living indicated by a house in the country and an income of £2,000 a year. I presume the Regent's Park Terrace ménage is beyond your new means ; so you had better at once look for a cheap room as near the British Museum as you can get it and arrange

31

with the landlady for your breakfast. Then select a cheap restaurant, or study the art of dining cheaply at Gatti's, for instance. Get a ticket for the Museum library, and study the drama there up to eight every night with all the advantages of communal heating, lavatory accommodation and electric light, with a comfortable seat, unlimited books, and ink and blotting-paper all for nothing. When you are settled in this groove with your necessary expenditure well within the fifty, write to your father and tell him that he may now cut off the supplies altogether ; excuse yourself pleasantly for having perhaps made a little unnecessary friction over the second Mrs. Tan—I mean Bright ; and wish him every domestic happiness and farewell. By cutting the cable before the supplies are exhausted you will prove that you are not merely making the best of a bad job, but boldly tackling the world as an independent man, in which character your father will not after be able to help respecting you. And I assure you you will write ever so much better after having shewn your mettle *to yourself* as well as to your father, who will begin to value you the moment you are able to do without him, possibly with favourable effects on his will, though I need hardly say that a calculation on that need not trouble a man of your years.

Excuse my giving you good advice : I have no doubt you get plenty of it. But what can I say on the case, as you put it to me, but what I have said ?

You are really too hard on Wilde. His " I have enjoyed myself very much " was an Irishman's way of giving all the credit to the actors and effacing his own claims as author.

All the paragraphs about Alexander having accepted a piece of mine are wrong. The only correct statement of the case is that in this week's *World*.

Yours sincerely,

G. Bernard Shaw.

29 Fitzroy Square, W.

22nd April, 1895.

Dear Mr. Bright,

As usual, my letters have been standing over unanswered for a long time ; and I am later than I intended to be in congratulating you on having so promptly and energetically faced and dealt with the situation created by your father's action. To tell you the truth, I was curious to see whether you would have stuff enough in you to tackle it ; for though it seems a simple matter enough, yet with a great many men—especially men of the artistic and literary temperament—a call for action ends like the first scene of the third act of Peer Gynt, where Peer sees the man chop his finger off to escape from military service.

"Ay, think of it—wish it done—*will* it to boot—

But *do* it——! No, that's past my understanding ! "

I congratulate you especially on the fact that all your friends and relations regard you as a madman. That is an indispensable beginning to a respectable, independent life

In your first letter you express yourself as rather staggered by my statement that a woman like Paula Tanqueray is the same at three as at thirty-three. That, however, is quite true. Rousseau dates his sexual susceptibility " from his birth," three years earlier than I have allowed for Paula. And there is no question of her being " corrupt, immoral in thought and idea " : that is begging the whole question of morality. She is different from Ellean ; but so is a poet different from a mathematician. If you take the mathematician's temperament as a moral standard, of course the poet stands condemned ; but why should you ? If you take Ellean as the standard, Paula is condemned ; but again, why not take Paula as the standard, and condemn Ellean as cold, unnatural, selfish and so on (which is what the Paula sort of woman invariably does) ? A critic must not take sides in this way without very careful consideration ; for it takes all

33

B

sorts to make a world ; and if you could make every woman a Saint Elizabeth, the result would be practically as disastrous as if you made every woman a Catherine II.

Your defence of Paula will not, I think, hold water. Let me remind you of it, by the way, as you have probably forgotten it by this time. You say, " She was, so far as study and observation can teach me, (not bad, Master Reginald, for a pure effort of your imagination) the daughter of a well-to-do, respectable man, probably a dignitary of the church. Chance threw her into the company of a fast set ; and moral ruin followed slowly but surely—facilis descensus Averni." But why did she join the fast set ? We are all thrown into the company of fast sets. We are all thrown into the company of slow sets too, and of religious sets, and political sets, and fashionable sets, and sporting sets, and gambling sets, and hideously debauched sets. But none of them rush at us and enlist us by a pressgang. We have to seek them out, to shew our sympathy with them, to make ourselves congenial company for them, before we can get into them. If Paula was the daughter of a dignitary of the church, it must have been far easier for her to become a district visitor or half a dozen other respectable things than a prostitute. Why, then, did she become a prostitute ? Because she was built that way, and for no other reason. I dare say your father is at this moment sorrowfully explaining to some friend that you were as sensible as possible at seventeen, and that you were well started at a City office, but that you unfortunately got into a set of theatrical loafers called the Playgoers' Club, and that they seduced you from the paths of business and corrupted you slowly but surely, and so on. But you know very well that the Playgoers' Club didn't come to you : you went to it because you are built that way, just as Paula went off in Mr. Jarman's yacht instead of going into Ellean convent, which was presumably equally within her reach. It is true that the whole female sex is driven towards prostitution or towards marriage for money (which is the same

34

thing) by economic pressure which, in the case of very poor women, is almost irresistible ; but that does not account for the difference between one woman and another in such matters, though it accounts for some of the difference between a man and a woman.

A remark of yours about the difficulties of indulging in a *Saturday Review* at a cost of sixpence a week suggests to me that you have not realised the advantages of Communism yet. At the Charing Cross end of St. Martin's Lane you will find a free library, with a newspaper room in the basement. You have nothing to do but walk in and read all the papers without any formality whatsoever ; and when you are done, you can go to the floor above and read all the magazines. We are trying to get a library for St. Pancras ; but we were beaten at the last poll. With the British Museum reading room round the corner, and this library within twelve minutes' walk, you are five hundred a year richer than Shakespeare.

I cannot bring myself to republish my articles. They appear very entertaining in the context of the events of the week in which they appear ; but just because they are good journalism, they are bad literature. I don't think the actress-manageress is going to do much good, because, obviously, she will want plays with good parts for the woman and bad parts for the men ; and so, though we shall have two sorts of bad plays instead of one —the actress-manageress' play at half the theatres and the actor-manager's play at the other half—we shall be as far as ever from the genuine drama. My preface is not an advocacy of the changes which I see coming, but simply a statement of them.

I shall go at Grein about the throwing open of the gallery at the I.T. If they really do that, it is a scandalous affair. Probably the truth is that the doorkeepers neglect their business and desert their posts.

Yours sincerely,

G. B. S.

29 Fitzroy Square, W.

4th November, 1895.

Dear Sir,

("Mrs. Warren's Profession")

Will you excuse an answer scribbled in a Metropolitan train. The paragraph you send me is (from its point of view) accurate enough. The actress alluded to is Mrs. Theodore Wright, to whom I proposed the part of Mrs. Warren. She was greatly startled when I read it to her; but the suggestion that she considered it a play that ought not to have been written will, I hope, be met presently by the announcement that she has consented to play the part. She has not done so yet, because she is only acquainted with the first two acts (an accidental visitor interrupted my reading of it to her); but she is, at any rate, quite open to consider it.

The play is a cold-bloodedly appalling one; but not in the least a prurient one. Mrs. Warren is much worse than a prostitute. She is an organism of prostitution—a woman who owns and manages brothels in every big city in Europe and is proud of it. With her gains she has had her daughter highly educated and respectably brought up in complete ignorance of the source of her mother's income. The drama, of course, lies in the discovery and its consequences. These consequences, though cruel enough, are all quite sensible and sober, no suicide nor sensational tragedy of any sort. Nobody's conscience is smitten except, I hope, the conscience of the audience. My intention is that they shall go home thoroughly uncomfortable. I can at least guarantee that any person who goes to gratify any prurient curiosity will be completely disappointed, as I am not a pandar posing as a moralist. The play has horrified everyone who has heard it, but only as an honest treatment of such a subject ought to horrify them. I want to make an end, if I can, of the furtively lascivious Pharisaism of stage immorality, by a salutary demonstration of the reality. Miss Janet Achurch at once offered to play the part of the daughter, in whom I have sought to put on the stage for the first time (as far as I know) the highly educated, capable, independent young woman of the governing class as we know her today, working, smoking, preferring the society of men to that of women simply because men talk about the questions that interest her and not about servants and babies, making no pretence of caring much about art or romance, respectable through sheer usefulness and strength, and playing the part of the charming woman only as the amusement of her life, not as its serious occupation. What do you think of that as a programme for a heroine ? To soften the prospect, I may add that her lover will be a youth of infinite charm, absolutely good-for-nothing, and absolutely pleasant. The Independent Theatre will find no difficulty in filling the parts. If the play were as vile as has been suggested, neither Miss Achurch or any other artist would touch it. Why should they, since it could do them nothing but harm ?

It may interest you to know that although I had little leisure during my autumn holiday in South Wales with the Sidney Webbs, I managed to complete a one-act play the hero of which is Napoleon Buonaparte—the Napoleon of the first Italian campaign, aged 27. The other characters are a strange lady, a sublieutenant, and an innkeeper ; and the whole is in the high comedy vein of "Arms and the Man." I have made no attempt to get it produced, as my position as dramatic critic makes it very difficult for me to take the initiative in any negotiation with our managers.

You can use all this information at your discretion, except that Mrs. Theodore Wright's name must be kept back until she has actually consented to play Mrs. Warren. Make an interview

37

of it if you like, though I should like a peep at it before it goes to press in that case, as I am writing in haste and without much consideration.

If you want to know anything about me at any time, don't hesitate to ask. I hope your plucky start has turned out well.

Yours sincerely,

G. Bernard Shaw.

29 Fitzroy Square, W.

11th November, 1895.

Dear Sir,

I must content myself with a hasty line. It is very possible that the Licenser will object to " Mrs. Warren's Profession." It is not as yet settled whether the I.T. will give an invitation performance of the play without troubling him (as was done in the case of " Ghosts ") or apply for a licence and risk the dropping of the project through his refusal. Until this is settled, I think the point had better not be raised. The date is not fixed ; but " Mrs. Warren's Profession " will come *after* " Little Eyolf," not before it.

All this overtime in the City is very objectionable from the point of view of health as well as leisure. For the moment I see no escape except by getting another berth, or some journalistic work.

As to what to read, read anything you feel curious about. It's quite possible that your real interest may not lie in the theatre at all. But in any case, read dramatic literature, not histories or criticisms of it. Read three or four of the most famous plays of Molière and Victor Hugo ; and sample Beaumarchais, Voltaire, De Musset, Angier and Dumas *fils,* until you know their styles. Read all Goethe's plays and a lot of Schiller's. Read a rhymed play of Dryden's, a play of Wycherley's, some of Congreve's, several of Sheridan, a Boncicault and a Robertson. Read Aleschylus, Sophocles, Euripides and Aristophanes (the Greek literature is very short). Get translations if you don't know the languages. Read them with a notion of their chronological order. Read Ibsen all through. Also Gibler's Apology and any memoirs of actors that you can unearth. That will do for a beginning. If you meet me anywhere, introduce yourself to me, if you don't mind.

In haste,

G. Bernard Shaw.

29 Fitzroy Square, W.

10th June, 1896.

Dear Bright,

No : there's no ring : there never really is. Since "Arms and The Man " I have written three plays, one of them only a one-act historical piece about Napoleon. The first of these was

" Candida " ; and there are obvious reasons for it's not being
produced—my insistence on Miss Achurch for the heroine, the
fact that the best man's part in it is too young for any of our
actor-managers (Esmond appears to be the only possible man
for it), and the character of the play itself, which is fitter for a
dozen select matinés than for the evening bill. The second—the
Napoleon piece—has practically never been offered to anybody,
because Ellen Terry took a fancy to it, and Irving proposed to
produce it and play Napoleon. But I want this kept strictly
private, as it may easily come to nothing, like other projects
that get talked over and are afterwards crowded out by the march
of events. The third play is only just finished. The only manager
who has seen it (in rough draft) is Daniel Frohmann, who is
perfectly friendly and is as likely as not to produce it in New
York if we come to terms, whilst there is no backwardness on
the part of our managers in wanting to see it. Considering that
my plays are difficult, that nobody believes there is much money
in them, that even their commonplaces—what you and I would
think their commonplaces—strike our managers as curiously
novel and advanced, and that all managers like to be courted a
little and are perhaps offended by the reticence which my position
as critic imposes on me in this respect—not to mention the
infuriating effect of my criticisms occasionally : taking all this
into account, I have nothing to complain of ; indeed, the wonder
is that they are so attentive and so interested in my attempts.
The fact is, the business of a manager is too desperately difficult
and hazardous to admit of any trifling with rings or the like.
Whatever Wyndham may have said or advised about a play not
his own, I have not the slightest doubt that if I brought him a
play tomorrow with which he could see his way to even three
months' good business, he would jump at it, though it were
calculated to send all the inmates of Marlboro' House into
convulsions. A manager is kept so desperately sharply to
business by the terrible drain of from £500 to £1,000 a week

going remorselessly on all the time, and his knowledge (derived from bitter experience) of how easily the receipts may drop from £100 a week to practically nothing, that he is forced to consider only what the public wants from him ; and if you find him giving them what they don't want, and withholding what they do want, you may always take the straightforward explanation that his judgment is at fault. It is true that in the theatrical profession people are always talking Machiavelli, so to speak, and devising imaginary diplomacies and boycotts and compacts and the deuce knows what not ; but at the first whiff of a success in prospect, all that is flung to the winds. The opinion of the Prince of Wales had absolutely no effect on "Arms and The Man." Nothing affected it, not even the cab strike. Every night some twenty or thirty pounds worth of people solemnly walked in and paid their money, the total receipts for the run being £1,777 (I always remember it because of the sevens). The cost was probably five or six thousand. The astonishing thing, to an outsider, is that this result, of which no secret has been made, does not really impress managers as being particularly disastrous: theatrical business means making one success pay for half a dozen failures, and the half-dozen failures seldom come off as well as "Arms and The Man " when allowance is made for the absence of a regular clientèle such as can always be depended on for a minimum at the Lyceum or Criterion. Wyndham, for instance (who has been very friendly to me), would probably look at it in this way. " If this fellow Shaw can pull in a couple of thousand pounds ' on his own,' and I can always pull in so much on *my* own, no matter what I play in, and the Criterion can always pull in so much of *its* own as a theatre with a reputation as a safe place to go for a jolly evening with people who don't know one author or actor from another, then, next time I run short of safe plays and am forced to risk an experiment, I stand to lose £2,000 less, in the worst event, than if I ventured with a quite untried man." But, of course, as long as he has

41

plays at hand with which he feels quite safe, he will not produce mine, which seem to him to be a quarter of a century ahead of the public. So you see, there is no more a ring against me than there is against Ibsen or Sudermann. Twenty years ago Grundy complained fiercely that there was a ring, because no manager would touch his plays as long as there was one by Byron to be had, or else the then inevitable adaptation from the French. Nowadays no manager will produce one of my plays as long as there is one by Grundy available—or Jones, or Pinero, or Carton, etc. Twenty years hence, if I prove a success as a dramatist, nobody will produce a play by a beginner of 1916 as long as there is a play by me on the market. There is no ring —there never is, never has been, never will be, although there always seems to be one to the younger generation battering at the door.

The news about " Mrs. Warren's Profession " is no longer true. There is no question of its immediate or remote production. The facts are rather funny, in a way. My first three plays, " Widowers' Houses," " The Philanderer," and " Mrs. Warren's Profession," were what people call realistic. They were dramatic pictures of middle-class society from the point of view of a Socialist who regards the basis of that society as thoroughly rotten, economically and morally. In " Widowers' Houses " you had the rich suburban villa standing on the rents of the foul rookery. In " The Philanderer " you had the fashionable cult of Ibsenism and " New Womanism " on a real basis of clandestine sensuality. In " Mrs. Warren's Profession " you had the procuress, the organiser of prostitution, convicting society of her occupation. All three plays were criticisms of a special phase, the capitalist phase, of modern organisation, and their purpose was to make people thoroughly uncomfortable whilst entertaining them artistically.

But my four subsequent plays, "Arms and The Man," " Candida," " The Man of Destiny " (the one-act Napoleon piece) and the unnamed four-act comedy just finished, are not "realistic" plays. They deal with life at large, with human nature as it presents itself through all economic and social phases. "Arms and The Man" is the comedy of youthful romance and disillusion, "Candida" is the poetry of the Wife and Mother—the Virgin Mother in the true sense, and so on and so forth. Now for the funny part of it. These later plays are, of course, infinitely more pleasing, more charming, more popular than the earlier three. And, of course, the I.T. now wants one of these pleasant plays to make a popular success with, instead of sticking to its own special business and venturing on the realistic ones. It refuses to produce "The Philanderer" (written specially for it) because it is vulgar and immoral and cynically disrespectful to ladies and gentlemen ; and it wants "Candida" or one of the later plays, which I, of course, refuse to let it have unless it is prepared to put it up in first-rate style for a London run on ordinary business terms. Consequently, there is no likelihood of any work by me being produced by the I.T., although "Mrs. Warren" is still talked of on both sides as eligible. You must understand, however, that we are all on the friendliest terms, and that I am rather flattered than otherwise at the preference of my friends for those plays of mine which have no purpose except the purpose of all poets and dramatists as against those which are exposures of the bad side of our social system.

Excuse this long and hasty scrawl. I let you into these matters because the man who gossips best in print about them is the man who knows what is behind the gossip.

Yours sincerely,

G. Bernard Shaw.

29 Fitzroy Square, W.

22nd September, 1896.

Dear Bright,

I have only just returned from the country for " Cymbeline."
I worked hard all through the holidays, but did not succeed in
answering my letters.

I enclose some press cuttings, which you may as well contradict in order to prove your omniscience to *The Sun*. The new
play, of which I gave you the first particulars, is entitled " You
Never Can Tell." Like all my plays, it contains some very
tempting parts, one of which has fascinated Cyril Maude. But
nothing whatever has been settled ; and the announcements
enclosed are altogether premature. The play is still in my hands ;
and you may safely conclude that it will remain there until it
leaves them for production. The decision of the Haymarket
management to produce a romantic play of the Zenda type
seems to indicate that they have reconsidered any notion they
may have had of a new departure in drama. At any rate, there
is one person who will not be surprised if " You Never Can
Tell " is produced elsewhere ; and that person is the author.

The question of the Napoleon play at the Lyceum will be
decided when " Cymbeline " is out of the way. I will let you
know as soon as there is anything to publish. As the matter
stands at present, Irving has made me an offer of which I have
no reason to complain. But I have proposed certain conditions
to which he is unaccustomed, and which he is perhaps slow to
understand, though they are of no particular consequence to
him ; and this has hung up the affair until there is more time
to consider it.

It was true enough about the bicycle accident. One afternoon
in the middle of July, I was riding in Pall Mall East when a

Great Western Railway van, coming out of the Haymarket, turned up Pall Mall on its wrong side owing to the horse shying at something, and charged me point blank. It was a pretty piece of tournamenting. I went ahead gallantly, and hit the horse fair and square on the breastbone with my front tyre, fully believing that the most impetuous railway van must go down before the onslaught of Bernard Shaw. But it didn't. I hit the dust like the Templar before the lance of Ivanhoe ; and though I managed to roll over and spring upright with an acrobatic bound just clear of the wheels, my bike came out a mangled, shrieking corpse. It was rather exciting for a sedentary literary man like myself ; but I gather from your opinion of my Bayreuth articles, the following week, that I was none the worse for it internally.

Yes : the *Star* articles on the International Congress were by me.

I very strongly advise you to practise public speaking : it will be of great use to you. If you look in the lecture lists in the Sunday papers, or in *Justice,* you will find plenty of announcements of meetings at halls and workmen's clubs about London or in the open air, where you can go and join in the discussion. I do not know what the debating societies, literary societies, and amateur local parliaments of today are—such things never last more than four years, and the ones I frequented are dead—but there must be as many of them about as ever. The Playgoers' Club is not exactly what you want ; but why do you not form a genuine debating society inside it ? If there are half a dozen young fellows who really want to talk out their opinions without the humbug of the big Sunday night celebrity hunting functions, they can easily agree to meet somewhere once a week, and take it in turns to get up a subject for discussion and put some work into it—not merely air their opinions and shew their cleverness, but work up some information for the use of the rest. For instance, Archer once delivered a series of lectures at the Royal Institution which contained a lot of information about

45

the development of the stage from the old platform in the inn yard to the modern picture stage. He might even consent to come down and talk for an hour to a little knot of fellows about it. As a rule, you will find that the better the man, the more willing he is to do a thing of that sort and the less disposed to waste his time on windy functions like the Sunday full-dress debates. However, that is by the way. Join or attend all the societies for discussion you can find, and speak every time, no matter how humiliating the result may be. Buy " The Chairman's Handbook " (or look it up in the Museum) so as to learn the technical order of public meeting. Most public men pick it up as they go along, and never to the end of their days know it properly ; but it is as well to be instructed in the matter, so as to be ready to take the chair if you are asked. From casual debating you might go on to delivering addresses ; and be sure you don't write them out or learn them by heart : make a few notes and speak extemporaneously from them. And don't despise or funk the street corner : it is an indispensable part of a speaker's education.

You ought to join the political association of your district, Liberal or Conservative, according to your opinions ; but you had much better begin as a Socialist and have a good, generous revolutionary time before settling down. Call at the Fabian office, 276 Strand, and tell Pease, the secretary, that you want to be advised how to begin. And bring a shilling to buy tracts with. If we are too slow for you, try the S.D.F. and serve a year or two under the red flag. You will make a blazing fool of yourself ; but you won't regret it.

G. B. S.

For : B. Shaw.

DURRANT'S PRESS CUTTINGS

Established 1880.   Chief London Office :—

57 HOLBORN VIADUCT, LONDON, E.C.

Advertisements and News received for all papers.

THE ST. JAMES GAZETTE

Dorset Street, Whitefriars, London, E.C.

(E. Southcott, Publisher)

Cutting from issue dated Sept. 18, 1896 :

"Rehearsals of 'Under the Red Robe' are proceeding vigorously, and it is expected that the Haymarket will reopen with that piece on October 15. We have already mentioned the principal characters of the cast, which is now completed by the engagement of Mr. J. L. Mackay (who, by the way, may be expected to blossom out as an author shortly) for the part of the Duc de Pombar, and Mr. Bernard Gould for that of the Lieutenant ; while Mr. Holman Clark is to appear as Clon, the dumb man. Among other pieces secured by Messrs. Harrison and Maude are 'Leoni,' a four-act drama by Mr. H. V. Esmond, and an entirely new play by Mr. George Bernard Shaw."

Close on Saturdays at 2 o'clock.

47

For : B. Shaw.

DURRANT'S PRESS CUTTINGS

Established 1880.   Chief London Office :—
57 Holborn Viaduct, London, E.C.

Advertisements and News received for all papers.

THE WESTMINSTER GAZETTE
Tudor Street, Whitefriars, London, E.C.
(Printed and Published by John Marshall)

Cutting from issue dated Sept. 19, 1896 :

" The new management of the Haymarket will start well provided with plays. In addition to ' Under the Red Robe,' with which the season will open, Messrs. Frederick Harrison and Cyril Maude have secured a new play called ' Leoni,' by Mr. H. V. Esmond, which will follow the piece founded by Mr. Edward Rose upon Mr. Stanley J. Weyman's novel. They have also accepted, for production later, a play by Mr. George Bernard Shaw, whose most diverting comedy, 'Arms and the Man,' will be gratefully remembered."

Close on Saturdays at 2 o'clock.

For : B. Shaw.

DURRANT'S PRESS CUTTINGS

Established 1880.   Chief London Office :—

57 HOLBORN VIADUCT, LONDON, E.C.

Advertisements and News received for all papers.

THE LIVERPOOL DAILY COURIER
Victoria Street, Liverpool.

(C. Tinling & Co., Publishers)

Cutting from issue dated Sept. 21, 1896 :

"Rehearsals of 'Under the Red Robe' are proceeding vigorously, and it is expected that the Haymarket will reopen with the piece on October 15. The cast is now completed by the engagement of Mr. J. L. Mackay (who, by the way, may be expected to blossom out as an author shortly) for the part of the Duc de Pombar, and Mr. Bernard Gould for that of the Lieutenant, while Mr. Holman Clark is to appear as Clon, the dumb man. Among other pieces secured by Messrs. Harrison and Maud are 'Leoni,' a four-act drama by Mr. H. V. Esmond, and an entirely new play by Mr. George Bernard Shaw."

Close on Saturdays at 2 o'clock.

29 Fitzroy Square, W.

25th September, 1896.

I have unluckily no news this week, as all appointments are put off until next, except one with Irving tomorrow. But as it seems that both he and the Haymarket people wish to hold on to the plays, and I cannot very well make difficulties if they are in earnest (which they now seem to be), you had better modify anything you may wish to say in the sense that the announcements in the St. James's, etc., were premature insofar as nothing has been finally settled, but it is likely that the news *will be* true by the time it is confirmed by the omniscient *Sun*. Say nothing about the Lyceum until the affair is quite settled.

G. B. S.

29 Fitzroy Square, W.

26th September, 1896.

Dear Bright,

I enclose the news. If you don't get it into tomorrow's *Sun*, you will be late, as Irving will give it to Bendall on his own account.

I have hastily thrown it into paragraph form ; so that if it comes in the rush of going to press you can send it to the printers without delaying to recast it.

I believe there was an Irving interview in the *Chronicle* (which I did not see) in which he referred to this play without naming me or it. He said, I understand, that I offered it to him ; but as a matter of fact I didn't, as I consider myself barred from that by my position as critic except in the case of managers who have taken the initiative by inviting me to shew them my plays. I don't want that said, but then I don't want the other things said either ; so if you can burke any statement about my offering plays uninvited, do so. It was Ellen Terry who managed the affair.

Observe that I have just declared that Irving has no literary judgment (see the *Saturday Review*). And on the same morning he accepts a play by me ! A neat dilemma—either my criticism is wrong or my play is bad.

Yes : bicycling's a capital thing for the literary man. I am delighted to hear of your holidays abroad instead of that cursed City office—I was once in an office myself. Also that you are now on your journalistic feet, and able to oblige me materially in letting my news out.

Let me give you a piece of advice. When a Shakespeare play is coming out—or a Sheridan one, or any old published one—buy a copy and *stage-manage* it for yourself, marking all the business. *Then* go and see it, and you will be astonished at the grip you will have of it and how much you will learn about the stage from your mistakes and *theirs*.

Yours ever,

G. Bernard Shaw.

29 Fitzroy Square, W.

23rd October, 1896.

Dear Bright,

The paragraphs last week were gorgeous, especially a slip at the end, which must have thrown all London for a radius of a mile round Mrs. P.C. into convulsions. You said she was to play Winifred Emery's MOTHER—Great Heavens, man : it's her *sister*.

The news now is that Ibsen is to the fore again. His new play is expected over in a few weeks ; and this has so waked his disciples up to the scandal of " Little Eyolf " being still unperformed, that Miss Elizabeth Robins has flung herself into the business with all her enegy ; and it may now be taken as settled that " Little E " will be produced before the end of November, at a series of subscription performances, with Miss Robins as Asta and Miss Janet Achurch as Rita, that is to say, with the strongest Ibsen cast yet seen in London. Echegaray is also to have a turn. I—G.B.S., *moi qui vous parle*—devoted nearly a whole article to Echegaray's " Mariana " when it was published here, and pointed out that it ought to be snapped up as a star part by some enterprising emulator of Bernhardt and Duse. Miss Robins has taken the hint, and promises " Mariana " after " Little Eyolf." She has also declared, in a signed circular, that if the performances produce any profit, she will use it as the nucleus of a fund for the performance of plays which are too good to be commercially practicable. This means, in plain English, that she does not believe in the Independent Theatre, and is going to set about its work as if it did not exist. In the face of its prolonged inaction *we* can only say " Serve it right " ; but what do Mr. Grein, and Mr. Charles Charrington, and Miss Dorothy Leighton say ?

Of course, this is nothing new for Miss Robins, to whose enterprise and devotion we already owe our acquaintance with "Hedda Gabler," "Karin," and "The Master Builder."

Yours,

G. .B. S.

29 Fitzroy Square, W.

9th March, 1897.

Dear Bright,

It seems to me that the facts—leaving the morals of the thing out of the question—shew that all attempts to meet demonstrations with counter-demonstrations only make matters worse, and that the right policy is to try to educate pit and gallery into dead silence and a prompt exit on the fall of the curtain (if not before) except when they feel pleased enough to clap a bit.

Here is a passage from a letter just received, signed E.H.S. :

"I hope you are not, my dear G.B.S., still smarting under the recollection of the first night of "Arms and The Man," when a galleryite raised his voice in protest against your making an ass of yourself by addressing the audience after the play. Do not imagine that *I* was the culprit, etc., etc., etc. etc."

In haste, your sincerely,

G. Bernard Shaw.

"YOU NEVER CAN TELL"

CAST

Valentine—a dentist (comedian—Wyndham style of part)
                                        Allan Aynesworth

Crampton—old man—strong part—the father...Brandon Thomas

The Waiter at the Marine Hotel—one of my finest creations
                                        Cyril Maude

McComas—solicitor to Crampton and Mrs. Clandon......Barnes
(Clandon is a *nom-de-plume:* Mrs. Clandon is Crampton's wife)

Bohun—an eminent Q.C. (only appears in last act,
        but very good character part).........................Kemble

Mrs. Lanfrey Clandon—Crampton's wife.........Fanny Coleman

Crampton's children—
        Gloria—her elder daughter—the heroine......Winifred Emery
        Dolly Clandon......⎰ very sparkling twins ⎱.........Eva Moore
        Phil Clandon........⎱   ⎰......J. L. Mackay

There is no plot. Mrs. Clandon is a woman of advanced opinions who has separated from her husband, a crusty, old-fashioned man, and brought her children to Madeira, where they have lived for 18 years. On her return to England with the children, now grown up, they meet the father, to whose anti-quated notions their modern ideas and advanced training are quite foreign. The play grows out of this incident. The four acts all take place on the same day. Place, the seaside (not further specified). Act I—In Valentine's operating room. Act II—Lunch on the terrace of the Marine Hotel. Act III—In the Hotel—afternoon. Act IV—In the Hotel—evening.

P.S.—My new play, "The Devil's Disciple," has been copyrighted this week for production in America by Richard Mansfield.

Private.   Lotus, Tower Hill, Dorking.

7th May, 1897.

Dear Bright,

I had better let you into all the mysteries of my plays. The fact is, nothing of mine is going to be produced at all. " The Red Robe " will probably be run through the season at the Haymarket ; and the public will be left to infer that it will be followed in the autumn by " You Never Can Tell." But the truth is that two of the leading parts proved too much for the resources of the Haymarket. The lady could not possibly have got through without strong support from the gentleman ; and the gentleman (your friend the dentist) was hopelessly beaten by his part, which would have required Wyndham or John Drew at least to handle it. So I went to Harrison and put it to him that we had better drop the business quietly. He was very loth to admit that such a breakdown could be possible, especially as the scenery was in hand and nine-tenths of the play shaping very cheerfully. But at last he recognised that the other tenth was out of the question. So we gave it up as a bad job ; and now " You Never Can Tell " is not likely to be seen until it is published. But I have settled with Harrison that this story is not to be published, as it would be very hard both on the actor who was cast for a part that was (as I foretold) quite beyond him, and on the others who could have done very well. We have simply said (truly) that " The Red Robe " has looked up again, and that the rehearsals of " You Never Can Tell " have been discontinued for the present. I let you into the secret so that you may know what you are about in the matter and not commit yourself to announcements that won't come off. But whilst you rearrange the background of your mind, don't let the public see anything.

Another collapse is over the Lyceum play. Irving declares that my article on "Richard III" meant that he was drunk, though, of course, the reasons he gives for publication are those in the enclosed press cutting. The statement that he has paid me a compliment and made me a present is, under the circumstances, enough to make a saint swear. In a few days, failing any friendly arrangement with Irving, I shall tell the whole story, probably in an interview in the *Daily Mail* ; and a very amusing story it will be. I shall have to do the interview myself, I expect ; but if you care to tell Springfield that you believe you can get an interview out of me on the subject, I shall bear you out unless Irving changes his attitude.

I enclose another sheet or two, containing as much as I want mentioned just now.

In haste,

Yours ever,

G. Bernard Shaw.

For : B. Shaw.

DURRANT'S PRESS CUTTINGS

Established 1880.　　　　Chief London Office :—

57 Holborn Viaduct, London, E.C.

Cutting from *Glasgow Herald,* dated May 4, 1897 :

DRAMATIC AND MUSICAL

" Sir Henry Irving has, I hear, relinquished his intention of playing Napoleon Bonaparte in Mr. George Bernard Shaw's one-act play, 'A Man of Destiny.' Sir Henry Irving had provisionally accepted the piece, but he now finds the character unsuited to him, and, moreover, as there is little chance of producing any half-programme work at the Lyceum for many months to come, he thought it best to return the manuscript to the author with, it is understood, a handsome compliment and a present. The story of Mr. Shaw's sketch is, it may be recollected, that of an incident in the first Italian campaign, when Bonaparte and other Republican officers endeavoured to secure some compromising letters from a seductive lady who was staying at a roadside inn. The part of the lady conspirator was to have been played by Miss Ellen Terry. It may now not impossibly go to the Haymarket."

Things you may mention.—Work it up as *news* in your own way, not as communicated by me to the paper in the first person —you will know how to manage it.

1. I have been elected a member of the St. Pancras Vestry. At the first general election of Vestries under the Local Government Act of 1894, it was urged that public-spirited men of some standing should come forward and offer to serve. I condescended to do this and was ignominiously defeated, my sympathy with Labour being considered disreputable by the workmen of St. Pancras. Now the Conservatives and Unionists and Moderates and other respectables of the parish have returned me unopposed in spite of my vehement protests that I have no time for such work. I recognise, however, that there is better work to be done in the Vestry than in the theatre, and have submitted to take my turn.

2. I have resolved to accept an offer made me by Mr. Grant Richards for the publication of my plays. I am not a disappointed dramatist, as the curiosity and interest shewn in my plays by managers, and their friendliness and accessibility for me, have exceeded anything I had any right to expect. But in the present condition of the theatre it is evident that a dramatist like Ibsen, who absolutely disregards the conditions which managers are subject to, and throws himself on the reading public, is taking the only course in which any serious advance is possible, especially if his dramas demand much technical skill from the actors. So I have made up my mind to put my plays into print and trouble the theatre no further with them. The present proposal is to issue two volumes entitled "Plays, Pleasant and Unpleasant." Vol. I, "Unpleasant," will contain "The Philanderer" and the appalling "Mrs. Warren's Profession" with perhaps a reprint of "Widowers' Houses." Vol II, "Pleasant," will contain "Arms and The Man," "Candida," and "You Never Can Tell." Possibly also "The Devil's Disciple" and "The Man of Destiny."

I decline to say anything more at present about Sir Henry Irving and "The Man of Destiny" except that the story, when I tell it—and I shall probably tell it very soon—will be quite as amusing as a Lyceum performance of the play would have been. None of the paragraphs in circulation convey the remotest approximation to the truth ; and the statement that Sir Henry has returned the MS "with a handsome compliment and a present" is a particularly audacious invention. This is enough for one week, I think.

29 Fitzroy Square, W.

13th May, 1897.

Dear Bright,

You will understand that dirty linen must not be washed in public, and that the most fatal character to appear before the public is that of a man with a grievance. So I must walk out of the Lyceum arm-in-arm with Irving.

I enclose you the conversational part of an interview, which you can fit with any introduction you please. I send with it one of the counterparts of the agreement alluded to in the interview ; so that you may have the evidence in your hand. Please return it.

The *Daily Mail* is, I think, the best mark for the interview, as Springfield invited me to speak myself on the subject in it. *The Star* also sent a man to me ; and the editor, Ernest Parke, is very friendly to me. I greatly regret that I am a day too late to have a copy of the interview in the hands of Clement Scott

before he writes his Saturday column (I wonder would the *D.M.*
give an advance proof for him) and of the other Saturday men.
However, it doesn't greatly matter. Make them put it in Saturday's paper at all events.

In haste, your sincerely,

G. Bernard Shaw.

During the last fortnight or so, no man has been so liberally
be-paragraphed in the Dramatic World as Mr. Bernard Shaw,
none more consistently abused on the one side, more assiduously
lauded on the other—and according as the taste of the writer
ran anti-Ibsen-wards or the reverse. Just as the announcement,
some eighteen months ago, that Sir Henry Irving had accepted
a one-act play entitled " The Man of Destiny " from *The
Saturday Review* set the town by the ears in amazement that
this most modern of the moderns, high priest to Ibsen and con-
demner of Shakespeare, had gained admission to the shrine of
the Lyceum, sacred to the memory of " W.S." ; so the statement, which has been current within the past few weeks to the
effect that the play is now once again in the author's hands, has
been the signal for many a tongue to start clattering. Wherever
two or three were gathered together, there the subject of
" G.B.S." and "A Man of Destiny " cropped up and, so surely,
one of the party would assume an air of mystery—wholly foreign
to his nature—and with some doubtful phrase as " I could and
I would " or " were I not in honour bound," assert that he
individually had some inner knowledge of the affair denied to
the meaner herd. This state of things was obviously destined

to end and, judging from the absolutely opposed statements scattered, that the psychological moment for an official pronouncement had arrived, a representative of this paper set out in search of the same. As the portals of the Lyceum, however, bear the Dante legend "All hope abandon, ye who enter here "—to journalists and seekers after ' copy '—his feet led him past Willington Street in a westerly direction to Fitzroy Square.

Having climbed innumerable stairs, knocked at a door and been cordially welcomed on the doormat, he subsided into the nearest available chair and, after a brief rest for recovery of breath etcetera, plunged in medias res with the query :—

"Can you be persuaded to say anything about the reports which have been circulating as to your Lyceum play ? "

"By all means. Do you want the history from the beginning ? " was the courteous reply.

"If you please, Mr. Shaw."

"Well, the matter is very simple. About eighteen months ago, when Sir Henry Irving was touring in America, one of my admirers shewed him a trumpery little one-act play of mine called 'The Man of Destiny.' Sir Henry, whose literary judgment is his weak point, enormously overrated the play, and made me an offer for it. I, of course, held the play at his disposal and made no further attempt to deal with it ; but I put the business off until he should have time to think twice about it. Nothing more passed until the night when he announced from the stage his intention of producing ' Madame Sans-Gêne.' I then represented to him that he could not very well play the two Napoleons—Sardou's and mine, and proposed that we should cry off. But I found him still obstinately under the spell of my genius. He saw no reason why he should not play the two—he had always wanted to play the young Napoleon—he had a medallion of him—he had looked like him in the last act of ' Claude Melnotte '—the part gave him what was missing in the older, coarser Napoleon of forty in ' Sans-Gêne ' : in fact, he gave me a thousand and one reasons for keeping to his resolution. I told him he overrated the play, and offered to write him a better one. He provoked me extremely by assuring me, with unmistakeable sincerity, that he was sure I should never write a better one : in fact, I think he was surprised that I had written anything so good. It was on this point that our main difficulty arose. Sir Henry Irving wanted to be free to produce the play when he could really do it justice by arranging for a run : I, on the other hand, declared that I had rather destroy the piece than have it produced as my latest achievement at some remote date when I had long outgrown it. In the end, he very reluctantly agreed to produce it before the end of the present year (this passed, you must understand, in July 1896 or thereabouts). A contract was drawn up : here it is ! "—and with this the portentious-looking document, full of legal technicalities, duly signed and witnessed by Miss Edith Wardell (Miss Edith Craig), was placed in my hands. " If you look through the clauses you will see that it is not an ordinary commercial affair. Sir Henry desired that we should deal with one another as men of honour ; and I accepted that basis gladly. You see !—there is no question of money, no advances, no penalties, a very modest fee (as such things go) for actual performances, payable out of the money paid by the public, and ample reservations to Sir Henry Irving of performing rights both here and in America, without any of the usual pecuniary considerations which attend such reservations. But, please, let it be clear that this is not due to any illiberality on Sir Henry Irving's part. He gave me practically carte blanche as to money terms ; but my position as a dramatic critic ties my hands in respect of advances and penalties, and prevents managers from objecting to special arrangements, which have a great air of being nobly disinterested on my part, but which are—as a matter of fact—inconvenient and exasperating in the highest degree to the unfortunate managers. You see then, that the agreement, though it effectually locked up my play, only bound Sir Henry Irving to produce before the end of 1897 ; and, by providing no penalty for non-compliance, left even that on the footing of an understanding, (in Sir Henry's own phrase) between men of honour. You may take the agreement away and study it if you like ; for I think it effectually disposes of the inventions which have been circulating recently as to the spirit in which Sir Henry Irving and I dealt with one another."

" But is the play to be produced, then, after all ? "

" No ! That is the second chapter of the story. The lapse of a year brings many disillusions with it ; and I suspect that when ' Madame Sans-Gêne ' brought Sir Henry Irving face to face with his rash engagement to play Napoleon twice, he began to realise what a piffling little affair this play of mine is, and how extremely difficult it would be to fit it into the Lyceum bill. Naturally, he has not recanted his former opinion of the play to me, whatever his private sentiments may be ; but after the accident which interrupted the career of ' Richard III ' and upset his arrangements for the season, we had a correspondence from which I gathered that, if I insisted on my pound of flesh in the shape of a production of the play this year, I should put him in a very disagreeable situation. His desire was that I should leave him free to produce it a little later, with a view to combining it with a certain play by one of our leading dramatists, which will create a good deal of interest when it is produced at the Lyceum. But I held to my old position, and preferred to settle the difficulty by cancelling the agreement, getting the play back, and crying off the whole bargain.

" Unfortunately, secrets in London are never more than half kept ; and before the conclusion of the matter left me at liberty to speak, a paragraph appeared stating that a play of mine had been rejected at the Lyceum. Immediately the cry was taken up on all hands and garnished with all sorts of ridiculous inventions. Our good old anti-Ibsenite grandmother, *The Era,* solemnly scolded the wicked people who had stated that plays by wicked people like myself were accepted at the Lyceum Theatre. A London correspondent, with a clever air of inside knowledge, described how my play had been returned ' with a handsome present.' One stupendous ass explained that Sir Henry returned ' The Man of Destiny' to rebuke me for writing excessively adulatory articles about him in the *Saturday Review.* All this nonsense seems to have created an appetite for a few authoritative words on the real state of the case. Well, you have them. Are you satisfied ? "

" Somewhat disappointed that we are not to see your play, Mr. Shaw."

" You need not be. My reputation as a dramatist grows with every play of mine that is *not* performed. Besides, Irving should go to the real Man of Destiny—Ibsen. 'A Doll's House,' ' Borkman,' eh ? "

The rest of Mr. Shaw's conversation was not directed to the Lyceum affair.

29 Fitzroy Square, W.

11th June, 1897.

Dear Bright,

I should not be surprised if " The Man of Destiny " were to take a trial trip at Croydon on the 28th, with Murray Carson as the one and only Napoleon. I don't know whether he has succeeded in fixing this, but I have given my consent ; and I am not aware that there are any special difficulties in the way.

Yours sincerely,

G. Bernard Shaw.

29 Fitzroy Square, W.

16th July, 1897.

The deadest secret of the week is that Mr. Laurence Irving has completed a five-act play which has produced such a powerful impression in the family circle that its production in an obvious quarter (not usually a likely one for young dramatic authors) has been privately determined on. Moral : do not make your deadest secrets the main topic of conversation at the Women's Jubilee Dinner.

You may safely venture on the above, or some paraphrase of it.

G. B. S.

29 Fitzroy Square, **W.**

11th March, 1898.

Unfortunately, I did not get a chance of acting promptly on your letter, as I was away when it arrived. I sent all the stuff on. It is much too long from the editorial point of view ; but they can select what they want. If they know their business they will drop the first half rather than the second. I have altered a few words, because the book in its present form has changed a little in its way through the press since I wrote to you. We hope to get it out by the middle of April : it is all passed for press now ; and nothing delays us but the American edition, which must, of course, appear simultaneously. Thanks.

G. Bernard Shaw.

Weekly Sun, March 20, 1898.

THE PLAYS OF "G.B.S."

———

Some Account of his Forthcoming Volumes.

(*Weekly Sun* Special.)

———

The polemics of Mr. Bernard Shaw—whether social, political, dramatical, or personal—are an unfailing source of delight to his readers, and even those who have writhed most under the heavy lash of his wit and invective have been known to join heartily in the general laugh against themselves. A sense of expectancy, therefore, hangs around the publication by Mr. Grant Richards a month hence of the critic-dramatist's collected " Plays, Pleasant and Unpleasant," in two volumes.

The familiar gibe, that publication is the last resource of the disappointed dramatist, will not hold water in this instance, for in at least two cases negotiations with West-end managers had reached the stamped agreement and rehearsal stages, only to be broken off at the eleventh hour. Perhaps, in his prefaces to these volumes, the author has seen fit to enlighten a mystified world on the subject ; but who shall prophesy ? You never can tell with " G.B.S.," who can be provokingly discreet when he chooses.

SHAKESPEARE'S LOST OPPORTUNITY

That the two volumes will be replete with startling innovations and split infinitives, everyone may well imagine, but I am now enabled to offer the public a more specific foretaste of the pleasures which await them. Like Ibsen, Mr. Shaw realises that, by disregarding the conditions under which managers labour and by throwing himself on the reading public, a dramatist is taking the only course by which any serious advance is possible. But unlike the Scandinavian, he has very decided views as to the futility of offering readers a mere reproduction of the " prompt copies " prepared for stage use. " The dramatic author must," he contends in one of these prefaces, " fall back on his powers of literary expression, as other poets and fictionists do. . . . What would we not give for the copy of ' Hamlet ' used

67

by Shakespeare at rehearsal, with the original 'business' scrawled by the prompter's pencil? And if we had, in addition, the descriptive directions which the author gave on the stage— above all, the character sketches, however brief, by which he tried to convey to the actor the sort of person he wished him to incarnate—what a light they would shed, not only on the play, but on the history of the sixteenth century! . . . It is for the want of this process of elaboration that Shakespeare—unsurpassed as poet, story-teller, character draughtsman, humorist, and rhetorician—has left us no intellectually coherent drama, and could not pursue a genuinely scientific method in his studies of character and society."

Having thus spelt "w-i-n-d-e-r" in the most approved Squeers fashion, "G.B.S." proceeds to the cleaning in his own style. The familiar stage directions and scenic specifications have been abolished, and in their places will be found finished —not to say ornate—descriptions, vivid character-sketches, psychologic notes and sallies of a characteristically mordant type.

SOCIETY THROUGH FABIAN GLASSES

Volume I consists of those plays which the author is pleased to term "unpleasant"—the unpleasantness lying in the fact that they convict the capitalistic phase of modern social organisation, and are written from the point of view of a Socialist who regards the basis of middle-class society as thoroughly rotten, economically and morally. Under this heading come "Widowers' Houses," "The Philanderer," and "Mrs. Warren's Profession."

The root idea of the first-named was the rich suburban villa standing on the rents of the foul rookery ; of the second, a four-act topical comedy, the fashionable cults of Ibsenism and " New Womanism " on a basis of clandestine sensuality—the Independent Theatre refused to produce it on account of its " immorality " ! ; whilst in the third, Mrs. Warren taxes society with her occupation.

The particular " profession " with which this lady is concerned is no less indecorous a one than prostitution. But she herself is far worse than a common prostitute ; she is a procuress, who owns and manages brothels in all the big European cities and is not ashamed of her trade. Her gains go to the respectable bringing-up of her daughter in total ignorance of the source of her mother's income. The crux of the drama lies in the girl's enlightenment and the ensuing consequences, which, though cruel and bitter enough to satisfy the most hardened " moralist," are all quite reasonable and sober. There is no dodging, on the part of the author, around the handy corner of suicide ; Mrs. Warren's conscience is not awakened to maudlin regrets of what she was at the age of sixteen ; and, in fact, it is all as remorseless and appalling as the ' Confessions ' of Rousseau, or the vivisection of womanhood by Schopenhauer. In the heroine will be shown the real New Woman, a highly-educated, capable, independent girl of the governing classes ; working, smoking, and unaffectedly preferring the society of men to that of women, because they talk of the things which interest her, and not of servants and babies, the ever-recurring evils of married life. Her peculiar charm is that she plays the part of the charming woman only as the amusement of her life, not as its serious occupation.

Volume II—" Pleasant Plays "—will comprise " Arms and the Man," the sparkling comedy, in three acts, of youthful romance and disillusion, which was the despair of the critics on its production at the Avenue in 1894 ; " The Man of Destiny," a one-act comedy, in which Sir Henry Irving had intended to appear as the youthful Napoleon ; "You Never Can Tell," a four-act modern comedy concerned with the adventures of a sparkling pair of twins ; and "Candida," a frankly sentimental play, which Mr. Shaw hopes to find appreciated by women, if not by men.

IN DEFENCE OF THE MANAGERS

It says much for his unfailing optimism that, despite the non-fulfilment of contracts, Mr. Shaw strongly combats the suggestion of that dramatic "ring" whose existence is so frequently deplored by Mr. Sydney Grundy. "There is no ' ring '," he asseverates vehemently, " there never really is. The fact is the business of a manager is too difficult and hazardous to admit of any trifling with ' rings ' or the like. Twenty years ago Grundy complained fiercely that there was a ' ring,' because no manager would touch his plays so long as there was one by Byron to be had, or the then inevitable adaptation from the French. Nowadays, no manager will produce a new man's play so long as there is one by Grundy available—or Jones, or Pinero, or Carton, or Louis Parker, etc. But why should an untried man be preferred to a tried one ? There is no ' ring '—there never is, never has been, never will be, although there always seems to be one to the younger generation battering at the door."

R. G. B.

29 Fitzroy Square, W.

7th April, 1898.

Dear Mr. Bright,

Thanks, yes : I saw your notice. The date of publication is fixed for the 15th inst.

There is a hitch about " The Devil's Disciple." The only theatre Waring could get was the Lyric, and that only conditionally, Arthur Roberts being in possession. If the business of " Dandy Dan " can be worked up to a certain figure, Roberts can hold on for the season : if not, Waring can come in next month ; but in the meantime it is impossible to make engagements and begin rehearsals. This cannot be explained definitely to the public, as, of course, the particulars about Roberts are confidential : all that can be said is that if the run of " Dandy Dan " closes in time for a new piece, the new piece will be " The D's D," and the actor-manager Waring. If, however, " Dandy Dan " holds out, it is not certain that I will consent to a production in October, because I have not had a day's real holiday for four years, and if I have to spend the autumn recess in town rehearsing, I shall risk a breakdown. And so all is uncertainty for the moment. The cast has been agreed upon ; but until the engagements are actually offered and accepted, it cannot be announced. But if you care to hazard an entirely unauthorised guess, your best selection would be Lena Ashwell, Hilda Hanbury and Mrs. Crowe, with Waring, Macklin, Bourchier, Playfair and Foss. But remember that I have no right to assume that any of these, except perhaps Macklin and Bourchier, will accept parts or be available. You must guess on your own responsibility.

G. Bernard Shaw.

THE LAND OF LETTERS

The Gospel of " G.B.S."

A Revolting and Dehumanising Document.

" If my readers do their fair share of the work, I daresay they will understand nearly as much of the plays as I do myself " —thus does Mr. Bernard Shaw encouragingly pat the public on the back, anticipating its contortions and discomforts, as he thrusts the formidable pill of his " Plays : Pleasant and Unpleasant " (two vols. London : Grant Richards) down its throat. The apologia was not unneeded, for this author's works are assuredly not for all markets—indeed, it is difficult to determine for whom he is purveying, since even " the unhappy prisoners of the home," revolting daughters to whom he claims to be the bearer of a message, may turn and rend the new evangelist for his caricatures of themselves. One fears, however, that the reverse may be the case, for the majority of women fatten on men's lies, and the liar whom they take to their hearts with the greatest fervour is he who, professing loudly that he understands the sex and the motives governing its actions, betrays every indication of never having passed the outposts. Where, for instance, has Mr. Shaw met the originals of Blanche Sartorious, Vivie Warren, Raina Petkoff, and Louka, the bloodless creations of his own ratiocinative temperament ? He may call them types of the advanced woman of today, but they are not, as he will find when he looks outside in the world for his material and not within.

Again, in regard to his male characters, Mr. Shaw may be " the voice of one crying in the wilderness," heralding the advent of some new Messiah, but his words fall meaninglessly to the ground because his ideas are expressed in insoluble terms of his own personality. " To be intelligible is to be found out," he may retort in the words of a fellow Irishman and wit, but the pertinacious presentment of himself as protagonist of each and all his works does not make for drama, but for sheer boredom and extinction.

.   .   .   .

The brain which can, in the course of five years, evolve seven plays of serious import by way of recreation from heavier work is, one unhesitatingly admits, abnormal ; the pity is that, with such opportunities and talents, Mr. Shaw should have elected to contrive everything in the same unpleasing mould of acrimonious psychology. He comes into the dramatic arena singularly well equipped for the fray ; he has a quick eye for striking situations, he is gifted with humour, wit, invention, and a power of expression of a very high order, but—fatal but !—he has no deep sympathy with humanity at large, and his overweening love of paradox leads him to see things through the wrong end of the telescope. In all his plays, with one exception (with which I shall deal presently), there is nothing helpful, nothing stimu- lating to the heart ; all is as drear and unsatisfying as the arid waste of the desert. And, though it is futile to expect idealism from one who is at no pains to conceal his contempt for it, we have at least the right to demand of the realist that he shall be artistic in his methods, which Mr. Shaw, unfortunately, is not. However true it might be of Mr. Wells's tentacular Martians, it is certainly false of average men and women to define their love either as an hysterical emotion or as a mere animal instinct dominated by sexual attraction ; and Mr. Shaw, in insisting on these as the only points of view, betrays the narrowness of his observation and the superficiality of his reasoning.

.   .   .   .

73

I have no space to deal at length with each separate play, but the last word on "Arms and The Man" and "Widowers' Houses" was spoken at the time of their production. Of the rest, "The Philanderer" is unspeakably nauseous, both in thought and expression, and the author's smiling self-satisfaction, as he plunges his hands deeper and deeper into the moral cesspool, is not the least revolting side of the business. He is said, by the way, to have spoken of this work as "dull filth unfit for human consumption," and it would be hard to find a more apposite description. "Mrs. Warren's Profession," though dealing with a most revolting subject, is a work of such amazing vigour and extraordinary power as almost to stupefy the coolest-headed. Even in his strongest scene, however, Mr. Shaw has minimised the effect in characteristic fashion. This is Vivie's comment on hearing that her mother is a shameful procuress, with establishments in all the great Continental capitals :—

"My dear mother,—You are a wonderful woman—you are stronger than all England, and are you really and truly not one wee bit doubtful—or—or—ashamed ? " Is this emotionless, sexless creature really typical of the true New Woman of today ? I trow not, though Mr. Shaw is at such trouble to make her consistent in her cold-bloodedness. "The Man of Destiny" is a prolix elaboration of familiar materials, the author having dramatised the quintessence of Taine's "Modern Régime." Napoleon's boast to Madame de Clermont-Tonnerre, "I'm always living two years in advance," is, however, scarcely justification for enabling him to foresee the rotten state of the English labour market in 1898, and his conviction of the Church Missionary Society, the capitalists, and the Forward politicians of today has apparently wandered into the play from some Fabian pamphlet. "You Never Can Tell" is as impossible, but not so skilful, as "Arms and the Man "—impossible, that is, in the strange admixture of drama, high comedy, and farce. The alternations from one to the other are as wonderful as a kaleido-scope, but the result on the mind of the reader is bewilderment and chaos.

· · · ·

There remains " Candida," and, for the sake of its purity and strength, one would willingly forget the remaining works—good, bad, and indifferent. It is because Mr. Shaw has, for once, not been ashamed to figure as a man of sentiment that he has succeeded in writing a really beautiful play where he failed before through excess of brainishness. In Candida he has depicted the real product of the New Woman movement—a noble-minded, graceful woman of dignity and resource, strong where her husband is weak, a Christian Socialist. The author's reasons for making the Rev. J. M. Morell, active member of the C.S.U., the Guild of St. Matthew, etc., a weak-kneed, windbag rhetorician are not obvious, but in every other respect the play is quite a faultless work of art. If only Mr. Shaw would give himself up more frequently to this mood, the reproach that we have no serious drama in England would soon be a gibe of the past.

· · · ·

But which way do his thoughts naturally tend ? " It was as Punch that I emerged from obscurity," he tells his readers in one of his diverting prefaces, and they may be driven to the belief that he prefers to go down to posterity in the same rôle. Certainly they will not lack material for this view, since, within a few pages of each other, he has made elaborate defences of such parasites on the modern drama as the Censor of Plays and the actor-manager. After that, he who would pluck out the heart of Mr. Shaw's mystery must own himself beaten, but no one can afford to neglect the attempt. These plays, both in idea and treatment, inaugurate a new departure, and, if anyone should fear for their reception in the theatre, let him take comfort from the author's paradoxical assertion that " it is quite possible for a piece to enjoy the most sensational success on the basis of a complete misunderstanding of its philosophy." On this assumption a fortune should be in store for the manager who would hazard the production of any one of these plays—save " Candida."

R. G. B.

Blen-Cathra, Hindhead,

Haslemere, Surrey.

15th Dec., 1898.

Telegraph Office : Grayshott, Hants.

Railway Station : Haslemere, 3¼ miles.

Dear Mr. Bright,

I was just wondering, when your letter came, whether it would be safe to send you a Wagnerite to your old address. I gather, however, that you have read that work. I wanted to send it because I thought a review which appeared in *The Sun* of my plays, signed R.G.B., a very promising one. Some of my " unpleasant " achievements horrified you a little ; and the fact that the feeling insisted on finding expression, and apt and forcible expression, when you would have probably rather liked to be complimentary, convinced me that you had not mistaken your profession. Of course, I didn't share your view of the plays : if I did, I should destroy them promptly ; but that, you will understand, is not the point. The thing is that, having something to say, you said it effectively, and got as far as a column without being superfluous. Further, you pitched into an author without offending him, a thing that can only be done by saying your mind quite sincerely. No doubt you have by this time found out for yourself that you can handle the pen a bit ; but it is always worth knowing how far that impression has been made on another party.

By the way, Napoleon's allusion to Manchester cotton is no anachronism. It would be one if made by Kitchener today ; but at the beginning of the century the new cotton factories of the industrial revolution were horrible dens of child slavery ; and Napoleon had heard all about them quite in the S.D.F. manner at the Jacobin clubs which he frequented in Paris before he got his chance at Toulon. You have no idea how old the ultra-modern revolutionary platform always is—indeed, the political platform generally. In my " Cæsar and Cleopatra," when it is published, you will find apparently outrageous gags in the aspect of allusions to the foreign politics of the Beacons-field–Salisbury period, which are nevertheless as " historical " as anything in Addison's " Cats."

I have no information to give you beyond this : that the play and " The Perfect Wagnerite " have been produced under great difficulties owing to my illness and my chapter of accidents. However, the play is now finished, except for the final revision and the arrangement of the stage business, at which I am at work now at the cost of a serious loss of ground in my recovery. It is in five acts, containing eight scenes, and involving considerable variety and splendour of mounting. It begins with the arrival of Cæsar in Egypt in pursuit of Pompey after the battle of Pharsalia, and ends with his departure after his six months' stay in Alexandria with Cleopatra. The whole episode was rejected by Froude as a mere romance ; but Mommsen describes it in considerable detail. The famous episode of the carpet in which Appolodorus the Sicilian conveyed Cleopatra into Cæsar's presence is introduced ; but in a way which would considerably astonish the French painters who are so fond of the subject.

Nothing whatever has been settled as to the performance of the play. Of course, " Cæsar and Cleopatra " suggests Forbes Robertson and Mrs. Patrick Campbell ; but they are not responsible for this, nor am I. I have read the first act alone to some friends in private, but to no one else. All announcements as to the destination of the play are premature : nothing has been proposed, nothing is pending. I shall take no trouble to get the play performed, as I shall be busy enough with its successor, which, with " The Devil's Disciple " and " C. & C.," will form my next volume of plays, and will certainly be published without any delay on the chance of production.

It seems an indispendable condition of my recovery that I should stop working. Yet I cannot escape. I *must* finish the play completely before the end of the year. Then I have an Italian Essay to write. Then a third play to complete my volume.

When you tell me of recovering in six weeks from a fall of 50 ft. and a broken leg, I can only envy you. My left foot has been hanging useless, with a hole in the instep, for eight months, and seems likely to complete the year, at least.

Put any of this information that you may care to use in your own words as usual.

In haste (my wife being exceedingly angry with me for writing after dinner).

Yours faithfully,

G. Bernard Shaw.

The Sun.

THE LAND OF LETTERS

_____

"THE PERFECT WAGNERITE"

AND SOME IMPERFECTIONS

_____

"How dost thou, Benedick, the married man?" We all know the crushing and witty retort of Signor Mountanto on Don Pedro, and Mr. Bernard Shaw's reply to the same (though unspoken) question will soon be as familiar. Under the comprehensive title of "The Perfect Wagnerite," he has contrived, amongst other things, a subtle, but cogent and glowing, panegyric of love as the noblest impulse in life, the crown of all earthly achievements. Of love the destroyer, love returned upon itself and blighting the possessor, he recks nothing. For him "God's in his Heaven—all's well with the world," and that suffices. The doctrine is old, prehistoric almost; but, emanating from a chartered cynic, whose fiercest diatribes have been directed against it in the past, it derives added weight. What a chastening effect it has had on the author, and on his style. "Where be your gibes now? Your flashes of merriment that were wont to set the table in a roar?" He who was used to rail at and condemn conventions is become their very slave; and his explanation of "Das Rheingold," through the medium of a delicious little allegory about "a young and good-looking woman" at Klondike before the gold fever set in, is a charmingly optimistic conceit after the best manner of Mr. Ruskin. That it should come to this! But, perhaps, I do wrong to take the cynic's conversion seriously. After all, adulation is the subtlest form of abuse, and this glorification of love and the married state may be the merest subterfuge. You never can tell with this author.

. . . .

" This book is a commentary on ' The Ring of the Nib-lungs,' Wagner's chief work. I offer it to those enthusiastic admirers of Wagner who are unable to follow his ideas, and do not in the least understand the dilemma of Wotan, though they are filled with indignation of the irreverence of the Philis-tines who frankly avow that they find the remarks of the god too often tedious and nonsensical." Having defined his position thus clearly, Mr. Shaw proceeds to envelop the hapless enthusiasts in still more impenetrable fogs of doubt and bewilderment. He becomes " all things to all men "—though scarcely in the apostolic sense. To those in search of know-ledge he is (professedly) a guide, philosopher, and friend ; over the superior person he exercises superiority ; upon the adept musician he pours out his vial of merciless scorn and contempt. You may have had the temerity to regard " The Ring " as the embodiment, in dramatic form, of sagas which the genius of Mr. William Morris cast in romantic moulds. If so, you are anathema to Mr. Shaw, whose least contemptuous definition of you is " ignoramus." After this, you will scarcely be surprised to find that, not only was Wagner an exiled revolutionist, but that his aim throughout his work was philosophically symbolic. And then—inevitably—are evolved from the dead man's brains philippics against greed of gold, " dangerous trades," established authority, statesmen, the survival of the unfittest, the application of the criminal code, Bryant and May's match factories, clerical shareholders in the same, " phossy jaw," and what not. For further points, vide labour leaders' speeches, passim. In fact, Wagner and his works are nothing more than a convenient wall behind which Mr. Shaw ensconces himself, and hurls forth a

Fabian essay of characteristic acumen and violence. The position is smilingly given away by the author's naïve reference, for further enlightenment, to his Fabian Society tract, "The Impossibilities of Anarchism." The worst of your Socialistic propagandist is his inveterate habit of establishing ethical signification in the work of every man whose cause he champions. The lengths to which this may go have recently been demonstrated by the publication of "The Tempter." One person, at least, is in no doubt as to the ethical signification underlying that niggling piece of blasphemous rhodomontade—Mr. Henry Arthur Jones, to wit. Mr. Shaw's polemics are all very dazzling, but is it Wagner? And are the difficulties of comprehension met by the knowledge that Alberic is not only a dwarf by birth, but in brain, typifying the millionaire capitalist, the sweating employer of labour, the foolhardy company promoter ; Siegfried, the saviour of Society ; Wotan, the ruler exercising dominion over credulous fools by sheer force of circumstances—not of birthright ? The promise of elucidation is delusive, after all.

.   .   .   .

But, though Mr. Shaw, as I have tried to show, had veiled a strong indictment against Society under a delusive title, he is not wanting in new ideas on the sempiternal question of Wagner's intentions. Quite the most daring of these is his contention that "Die Götterdämmerung" is a thorough grand opera, in support of which he adduces internal evidence to prove that, although played as the last of the tetralogy, it was in reality conceived first. The apple of discord he cheerily casts into the musical arena, and smilingly awaits the dilemma of some new Paris. Heaven forbid that I should pick it up ! Mr. Shaw says the last word on the vexed point—was Brynhild ravished on the mountain-side, and, if so, by whom ?—though sentimentalists will view with alarm the restoration of her virginity at the price of perjury and murder. He also advances Wagner's explanation of his own work, which, however,

81

necessarily falls short of G.B.S.'s, and, in conclusion, pleads strongly for the establishment of a Wagner Theatre and Festival in London. This is, indeed, one of his few moments of earnestness in the whole book. May one hope that in his next book Mr. Shaw will descend still further towards his public ? To pile an Ossa of bewilderment upon a Pelion of mystification baffles and disheartens the student, who would understand his tutor if only the latter were more considerate in his use of a superior intellect. Meantime, no professing Wagnerite—and who in these days is not ?—can afford to neglect this commentary on " The Ring." It may upset preconceived ideas, and occasionally annoy the reader by sheer force of egoism ; but, as a piece of well-reasoned criticism, it does for music what Mr. Ruskin did for Turner in " Modern Painters," and it is written in Mr. Shaw's most brilliant and attractive style.

R. G. B.

23rd October, 1899.

S.S. Lusitania.

I have left Hindhead : please cancel that address and fall back on 29 Fitzroy Square, W., or 10 Adelphi Terrace, W.C. Nothing is settled about the D's D : M.C. only had my licence to perform it at Kennington until my return on the 30th inst. I am not in any attitude about it : it is available for any manager who wants it. Yes : " Captain Brassbound's Conversion " is the third play I mentioned to you. It was written for Ellen Terry, not for Sir H.I. ; and she will possibly produce it independently ; but this is not to be taken as indicating any rupture at the Lyceum. Miss Achurch asked Harvey to play the poet in " Candida," not Morell. He refused. Forbes Robertson is not going to produce " Cæsar." He had the refusal up to last May, when he definitely decided not to venture on it. But as you know, all these decisions mean as little as the opposite decisions which give rise to them. You may safely contradict every state-ment you see in print about my plays. They are all nonsense.

G. Bernard Shaw.

FOR INFORMATION ABOUT THE STAGE SOCIETY, APPLY TO FREDERICK WHELEN, CARE OF GRANT RICHARDS, 9 HENRIETTA STREET, COVENT GARDEN.

10 Adelphi Terrace, W.C.

2nd May, 1900.

Dear Bright,

The Three Plays for Puritans will be published next autumn. There will be quite a collection of prefaces, chief among them a tremendous sermon entitled " Why for Puri-tans." In it I give, with exceeding frankness, an account of the London theatres as I found them during my critical campaign on the *Saturday Review* from 1895 to 1898, when I collapsed and nearly died of pure inanity and emptiness administered by the managers in large weekly doses. I appeal, of course, to the Puritans to come to the rescue of the stage ; and to shew that this is no mere personal eccentricity of mine—no hackneyed Shawism—I find, whilst my preface is still in MS, William Archer in the *Morning Leader* crying out for a new Collier to write a new treatise on " the profaneness and immorality, etc.," and Massingham immediately afterwards hotly defending George Moore against Walkley from the Puritan point of view.

In a second preface I attack the current critical chatter about the so-called originality of my plays, shewing that the peculiar Diabolonian creed of the " Devil's Disciple " is as old as William Blake, and had been freshly affirmed by Robert Buchanan in a poem published before the D's D was written ; that the contrast between mere knighthood and military capacity which is the theme of "Arms and The Man " was elaborated years ago in Mommsen's History of Rome, one of the best-known books in Europe ; that Buchanan was quite right in pointing out that my stage tricks are as old as Charles Mathews in " Cool as a Cucumber," and probably centuries older ; and that, in short, it is only the criticism that reads nothing, remembers nothing, and knows nothing, that is astonished and bewildered by my sallies.

A third preface deals with Shakespeare, and with epoch-making authors and artists in general, explaining my view that Shakespeare's epoch is over.

I have not yet written any more prefaces ; so it only remains to say that the book will conclude with an appendix consisting of the three plays—" The Devil's Disciple," " Cæsar and Cleopatra," and " Captain Brassbound's Conversion." Publishers : Grant Richards and H. S. Stone & Co. of Chicago.

Now as to yourself. *Your* danger is not failing to get work, but getting too much. Journalism, when it gets hold of a willing and capable horse, walks him to death at forty, and leaves his ghost walking painfully for another twenty or thirty. All you can do, of course, is to blaze away ; but in as far as you can economise yourself, do. Editorships, which are the prizes of the profession, are frightfully precarious—witness the case of Massingham. Try and fire off a book or two, or get a personal hold of the public in some way, unless you become as strong in the special journalist's art of knowing the public and picking the writers as to be unassailable.

In haste,

Yours ever,

G. Bernard Shaw.

10 Adelphi Terrace, W.C.

2nd November, 1900.

Dear Golding Bright,

Now that the Borough Council election is over, I can snatch a moment to answer your letter. " Three Plays for Puritans " is passed for press at last, though the effort has almost slain me ; for you will observe that I have had not only to fight the municipal election, but to write " Fabianism and the Empire " in the throes of the General Election before that. I have had, I need hardly say, no holiday. But the elections are over at last (though demands for speeches in connexion with the School Board and County Council elections are dropping in already) ;

and the book is only waiting for the printing of the American edition and the reproduction of an Italian photograph of the mosaic in St. Mark's representing the lighthouse of Alexandria. That is, of course, for " Cæsar and Cleopatra." There will also be a portrait of Cæsar from the Berlin bust (our famous British Museum one has been given up at last as unconnected with Cæsar), and a portrait of General Burgoyne (for " The Devil's Disciple "). Just observe, if you please, what these volumes mean. A play costs two or three times as much real work as a novel, which involves nothing but inkslinging. Yet I give an ungrateful public *three* plays in a volume, besides prefaces, notes and sermons without end. When I say *give* I mean give ; for the book will not yield me dock labourer's wages for the mere manual toil it costs. This one has really three prefaces, entitled respectively " Why for Puritans ?," a criticism of the contemporary theatre, " On Diabolonian Ethics," explaining the foundation of " The Devil's Disciple," and " Better than Shakespeare ?," in which I clear up all that confusion to which you allude about Greek methods and Shakespeare's epoch and so on.

" Captain Brassbound's Conversion " will be produced privately by the Stage Society in December if it can be cast— an open question at the moment. " The Devil's Disciple " is coining money in the provinces in the hands of Forbes Robertson : its production in Dublin the other day seems to have been furorious.

No more news at present : I do not even know yet whether I am elected for the Borough Council or not. If not, the relief will be enormous, and the dramatic output of next year a good deal bigger.

Yours sincerely,

G. Bernard Shaw.

10 Adelphi Terrace, W.C.

12th December, 1900.

Dear Bright,

In St. Pancras we prosecute disorderly houses with great assiduity; and I have handed your letter to our leading Purity man to stimulate him to further exertions.

But what is the use of all that, except to make brothels less noisy and policemen more heavily tipped? In St. Pancras a railway porter's wife, to whom five shillings a week added to her husband's wages make all the difference between plenty and penury, will do char work for that sum to make it the standard price of a woman's labour in the district. Imagine what that means to the single woman or the widow with children. Suppose you were a young woman and had to choose between such starvation for honest work and picking up a shilling in Alfred Place or five in the Euston Road, how would you feel towards people who were quite satisfied to sweat you for twelve hours for a shilling, but would not hear of their sons being "solicited"? Read "Mrs. Warren's Profession" again. Everybody should read it carefully through once a month. If they did, we should get something better than virtuous indignation brought to bear on the subject.

"Three Plays for Puritans" will not be out until January. No advance copies as yet. You shall have one when they are ready.

Yours ever,

G. Bernard Shaw.

10 Adelphi Terrace, W.C.

5th April, 1901.

Dear Golding Bright,

I had better not give you an introduction to Frank Harris :
he is not accessible in that way (very few men are, by the way).
You had much better go at him on your own account. Tell him
what has befallen you on the other papers, and say that your
only chance is to find a strong editor. He may not find it at all
easy to pitch on a dramatic critic. At all events, there is no
harm in trying, provided you don't try to force his hand with
an introduction.

The address for the new paper is 64 Victoria Street, S.W.—
at least, he has just written to me about it from there.

I have no intention of returning to regular journalism—no
time for it.

Just off to Provence to recruit : I haven't had even a Sunday
off since October, '99.

Yours sincerely,

G. Bernard Shaw.

10 Adelphi Terrace, W.C.

6th April, 1901.

Dear Golding Bright,

Your letter, addressed most absolutely to Hindhead (now two years out of date), has only just reached me. Here is what you want about Carnegie.

All I can say is that if Mr. Carnegie proposes to be guided by a committee of critics, actors, actresses, managers, and students of the stage, the sooner he is made a ward in Chancery and strictly looked after, the better. Probably what Mr. Carnegie really said was that the committee should *not* include any critic, actor, actress, manager, or proposed student of the stage. If Mr. Carnegie is a wise man, he will buy my three volumes of plays and read the prefaces very carefully. He will have to provide himself with some small change, however, as I do not issue a five-million-dollar edition. I refer him more particularly to the preface to Volume II, " Pleasant Plays," in which I shew how a preliminary experiment can be tried in a businesslike way by inviting a manager of established competence to undertake a series of performances of selected plays with a guarantee to protect him against pecuniary loss. This would provide the first thing wanted : a repertory, and a company. If any play produced under these conditions proved a great popular success, the manager could immediately transfer it to his ordinary popular programme. Finally, he might take a separate theatre, or build one, for the endowed repertory ; and that theatre might possibly soon have a steady clientele which would make it independent of any guarantee. In Mr. Carnegie's place, I should make this proposition to Mr. Alexander in London and Mr. Mansfield in the United States, and see how it worked for a season or two.

I repeat, it might prove so successful that a permanent endowment would be quite unnecessary—that a start is all that is required.

For permanent endowment, I should reserve such a scheme as Mr. Alexander has suggested, of a school of physical expression and rhetoric attached to the London University, and available for the personal training of clergymen, barristers, naval and military officers, and all persons who have to speak or command in public, including, of course, actors, but no more specialised for actors than for theologians or jurists. The first qualification I require from an actor is that he shall be able to impress the back row of the gallery with his speech and bearing ; and that is what the captain of a P. & O. steamer requires also from his third officer. And there are a hundred departments of business in which this personal training is as important as in the professions. My famous curate who did not know the difference between a collect and a gargle is not the only man in the world whose career is wrecked and whose work is spoiled for want of the physical drill of rhetoric.

Finally, there remains for permanent endowment the municipal theatre : the chief art department of our rapidly-developing Collectivism. I shall have something to say about that when the preliminary experiments I have suggested are settled ; for the present it would take too much of your space and my time.

You may as well put the above into the *Express* as it stands : it may do something to shape the nebula.

Yours,

G. Bernard Shaw.

10 Adelphi Terrace, W.C.

6th November, 1901.

Dear Golding Bright,

I have just received a letter from the Stage Society concerning " Mrs. Warren's Profession." It says :—" Miss Fanny
Brough withdraws : she was under a misapprehension, it
appears, and accepted a part in a play by you not knowing
anything about the particular play."
You may take it as a safe rule that everything that is settled
about the Stage Society will be unsettled next day.

Yours,

G. Bernard Shaw.

Piccard's Cottage,   10 Adelphi Terrace, W.C.

St. Catherine's,   8th November, 1901.

Guildford.

Dear Golding Bright,

When I gave you that advice what was in my mind was that
you were as likely as not to marry your landlady's daughter in a
fit of sentimentality. I did not foresee that you would rush so

91

violently to the other extreme as to marry George Egerton. How do you like it ?

" Mrs. Warren," if produced at all, will be produced on the 8th December and repeated, as usual, on the 9th. Fanny Brough will play Mrs. Warren, and Miss Mackintosh Vivie : Granville Barker will probably play Frank : the rest of the cast is too conjectural to be stated yet. It is quite possible that the performance may fall through owing to difficulties about the theatre ; but we must assume for the present that the play is going to be done, and treat its abandonment, if abandoned it be, as a separate piece of news for subsequent publication.

My municipal work is certainly interfering very seriously with my dramatic activity ; but I have a new play in hand for all that.

Yours sincerely,

G. Bernard Shaw.

10 Adelphi Terrace, W.C.

30th November, 1901.

Dear Golding Bright,

The story of " Mrs. Warren " may as well be advanced a stage further, now that Mrs. Langtry has repudiated so indignantly the statement (which nobody made) that the performance was going to take place at the Imperial Theatre.

It is quite true that Miss Fanny Brough, on learning the nature of Mrs. Warren's profession, revoked her consent to play. But it is also true that on Miss Fanny Brough's proceeding to read the so-called wicked play, she energetically and enthusiastically withdrew her objection, resumed the part, and will, I guarantee, very considerably astonish two classes of people in it : namely, those who are now scribbling about the play without having read it, and those (mostly managers) who are under the impression that Miss Brough is only a comic actress.

The truth is, there has been a rally round the play which has astonished me. I opposed its production by the Stage Society on the ground that it might expose the manager of the theatre to the resentment of the Censor, who has, unhappily, committed himself to the old censorial position that illicit sexual relations must not be mentioned on the stage unless, as in the case of the Dame aux Camellias, Zaza, and Iris, the heroines of them are made extremely attractive, so as to offer the largest possible inducements to poor girls in the gallery to follow their example. As it is clear that Mrs. Warren will not make a single convert to the cause of Polyandry, the King's Reader of Plays will not tolerate her ; but even his department has gone so far as to disclaim any cognizance of a performance which will be open to the public for payment at the doors. Still, I urged the Society to let it alone, and suggested the substitution of my fully authorised and licensed play, " The Philanderer." But the Society strongly objected to the morale and tone of " The Philanderer," and overbore me as to Mrs. Warren. They would have it ; and the cast would have it ; and, in short, I had to withdraw my prudent objections in some disgrace, which served me right.

There has been no difficulty whatever with anyone, save only the Censor and Mrs. Langtry, on the score of the play's character : quite the contrary. I had no suspicion that the play had made such an impression, though I, of course, knew from its reception by the reviewers on the publication of " Plays, Pleasant and Unpleasant " (to the horror of the then young and innocent R.G.B.), that there was danger of its being misunderstood as a mere impropriety. You will see by the letter from the National Vigilance Society in *The Times* today that Mrs. Warren is as busy and prosperous as ever in real life, in spite of all the committees that have been formed throughout Europe to suppress her. Alfred Place and its neighbourhood is as crowded as ever with knots of women ; and it is still not possible to say truthfully to one of them that she will be better treated and better paid by Society if she turns " honest " and takes to charwoman's work at the St. Pancras standard of five shillings a week.

The cast is : Mrs. Warren—Fanny Brough ; Vivie Warren—Madge Mackintosh ; the Reverend Samuel Gardner—Charles Goodhart ; Frank Gardner—Granville Barker ; Praed—Julius Knight ; and Crofts—tell you later on, as we are changing.

You will observe that none of these people have any inducement to play except the purely artistic inducement. They won't be paid ; and they are not nobodies or novices. Their names and positions, and those of the Committee of the Stage Society, are sufficient cards to play against the view to which the Censor has lent his countenance.

The sole obstacle to the performance is the intimidation of the Censor, and his absolutely autocratic power—to ruin any West End manager who offends him, without reason given or remedy available. But though he cannot divest himself of his powers, he has, to do him justice, disclaimed, as far as he officially can, any concern with private performances. And the disclaimer has been made in reply to an inquiry in connection with this performance and this play. It is still probable, however, that the performance will take place out of his jurisdiction.

All of which information I recommend to your best discretion in case you should be dealing with the subject in the

Daily Express or elsewhere. It must figure as your own information, because I am not justified in making any official communication to the press without consulting the others ; so this must be matter come to your private knowledge.

Yours,

G. Bernard Shaw.

10 Adelphi Terrace, W.C.

6th December, 1901.

Dear Golding Bright,

" Mrs. Warren " is postponed to next year. The cast was complete—Charles Goodhart as Crofts and Cosmo Stuart as the Rev. Sam Gardner—and the last difficulties surmounted, when Miss Halston (my Strange Lady in " The Man of Destiny " and the original Gloria in " You Never Can Tell ") fell ill. Now Miss Halston is touring with Alexander ; and as Miss McIntosh is also in the Alexander tour she had to take up so much of Miss Halston's work that she could not go on rehearsing Vivie Warren. So we had to give in. Probably the postponed performance will be early in January. It must be early, as Granville Barker's " The Marriage of Anne Seete " is announced for the 19th and cannot be postponed.

I will call the attention of the S.S. to the omission of the *Express* from their press list. It must be accidental—probably due to compiling the list from an old press guide dating from the pre-*Express* era—as we need the press to encourage actors to play for us. They get nothing but their notices.

Yours,

G. Bernard Shaw.

PRIVATE

P.S.—The par. in the *Express* was excellent. Miss Brough, before I had seen it, terrified me by telling me that it stated that she was playing because she had "the courage of her opinions." ! ! ! !

10 Adelphi Terrace, W.C.

23rd February, 1903.

Dear Golding Bright,

Are you going to Vienna to see the first night of "The Devil's Disciple" (Ein Ieufelskerl") at the Raiemund Theatre, with Wiene as Dick Dudgeon and Thaller as Burgoyne? Of course not. Neither am I. But that first night is fixed for the day after tomorrow—Wednesday the 25th.

The Censorship has stepped in and forbidden (for the present) the production of "Arms and the Man" ("Helden") at the Burg Theater, Vienna, because of the political excitement about

Macedonia and Bulgaria. People who thought that the play was comic opera and not history will now, I hope, hide their diminished heads.

In Berlin there is another row over "Arms and the Man." The Social-Democratic Stage Society of Berlin (the Freie Volksbühne) want to perform the play; but Paul Lindau objects strongly on behalf of the Deutsches Theater, at which the play is to be produced in the regular way. The Social-Democrats say that they cannot be prevented from giving a " private " performance of a play by a world-renowned Socialist. Lindau threatens legal proceedings. The author and the translator (Siegfried Trebitsch) play Spenlow and Jorkins, Shaw declaring that he prefers a Socialist audience because his plays are intended for exceptionally intelligent people, but that Herr Trebitsch (Mr. Jorkins) must be consulted in the matter; and Trebitsch regretting that his contract with Herr Lindau makes it impossible for him to comply.

" Candida " has been secured by the Dresden Hoftheater. All this means that Trebitsch's translations of " Candida," "Arms and the Man," and " The Devil's Disciple " have made a sensation in Germany, where the English drama has hitherto been utterly despised, and that there is a Bernard Shaw boom on in the Kaiser's realm and in Austria.

I write you this as Trebitsch will be grateful if it gets into the English papers; and it occurred to me that it might help you to pad a column. It is quite fresh: I have not mentioned it to anyone else.

Yours ever,

G. Bernard Shaw.

10 Adelphi Terrace, W.C.

15th April, 1904.

Dear Golding Bright,

Daly's project is utter lunacy : he would get nothing by it but a load of debt that would cripple him for the next ten years. I have written to him like a father about it ; and he knows by this time that I shall not withdraw " Candida."

Our business is to keep him quiet ; so that he may produce " You Never Can Tell " next season in New York and make a solid success of it. There is not much gilding on " Candida " gingerbread except for the author : there is not much to be made out of £450 a week by any manager, even with the cheapest play on the stage.

Yours ever,

G. Bernard Shaw.

32 Via Porta Pinciana, Rome.

13th May, 1904.

Do you know anything of an American actress named Miss Grace Filkins (Mrs. Marix) ? She wants to play " Captain Brassbound's Conversion," and says she has just the right position on the stage for it. Unfortunately, I've never heard of her. Have you ? Or has Miss Marbury ?

G. Bernard Shaw.

10 Adelphi Terrace, W.C.

28th June, 1904.

Dear Golding Bright,

Daly is coming here at 1. Tell him that you have no instructions but that you understand that his plan of producing " You Never Can Tell " next winter and " Mrs. Warren's Profession " in the spring is quite agreeable to me and that you have no doubt that I will give him an agreement on the " Candida " terms if he asks me for it. Be kind to him ; and when he occasionally explains (under the impression that he is the author and owner of my plays) what he will do with them, or allow or disallow to be done with them, in America, do not attempt to cure him of his delusion, as his enthusiasm will be all the keener for his believing that the works are his own. He is a likeable lad.

Thanks for Miss Rehan's address.

Yours ever,

G. Bernard Shaw.

The Old House,   10 Adelphi Terrace, W.C.
    Harmer Green,
        Welwyn, Herts.   3rd July, 1904.

Dear Miss Marbury,

I have seen Miss Rehan, and read the play to her. The result is quite satisfactory : she is converted and enthusiastic. She says she is engaged by Shubert for 16 weeks. I have promised to wait as long as she likes. She wants to play it both in London and America. That is all, so far. She looks fine, and will be as good as ever she was in a play by

Yours ever,

G. Bernard Shaw.

The Old House,   10 Adelphi Terrace, W.C.
    Harmer Green,
        Welwyn, Herts.   5th July, 1904.

I should very greatly prefer a London production of " Brassbound " in the first instance, as I could then rehearse it myself. It is better to take a play from London to New York than bring it from N.Y. to London. If I could arrange this for next spring I should make Miss R. hold her hand this winter. Frohman is the man for it, and he should engage Drew to support him. Do nothing until you hear further from me. I am pulling the wires tentatively.

G. B. S.

The Old House,   10 Adelphi Terrace, W.C.
   Harmer Green,
      Welwyn, Herts.   28th July, 1904.

The Stage Society is compiling a list of " the following plays are under consideration " for its prospectus of next season. A play by George Egerton would add to the decoration considerably ; but nothing of the sort has arrived yet. Has the distinguished author changed her mind ?

Tell Loraine that in consequence of the distressingly high standard of sanity among managers, the demand for " Man and Superman " is deplorably slack. Even Daly has not mentioned it.

G. B. S.

Address telegrams to   10 Adelphi Terrace, W.C.
" Socialist London."
                  27th October, 1904.

Dear Golding Bright,

I cabled direct to Miss Marbury last night to say that I would not take 700 dollars a week for " Man and Superman " from Mansfield, but that I would take 960 dollars or 120 dollars a performance. I was screwed up to this pitch of avarice by a glance at the returns in 1898 from " The Devil's Disciple," which made seven hundred dollars seem paltry. Further, I said that I preferred my 10%. I also signified that she ought to try Loraine, if only to put a stop to his idiotic cabling to Green Street with

101

Miss Marbury within five minutes' walk. What the devil does he mean by it ?

You may tell all and sundry that " Candida " is not in the market for this winter. I have resolved to keep it until it has been worked up a bit more in London.

Tell Miss Marbury that the Irish play is a peculiar product, and might possibly lead to lynching if exploded on an excitable Irish population in a lawless country like America. I promised to let Daly have it if " You Never Can Tell " fails and leaves him stranded. I read a bit of it to him, and was struck by the way in which he caught hold of it.

Daly, by the way, has gone out of management on his own account, and has signed himself into slavery to Liebler & Co. for five years. He says he is to have " supreme charge back of the stage as regards the selection of the plays, players, etc." This may be good news and it may be bad. Ask Miss Marbury which.

I am much applied to from America just now to lecture. Both Daly and Shubert have this idea. I never like to say no : so tell Miss Marbury to say, if they ask her, that I am a very good lecturer, and that my terms are a million dollars for a tour, not including the salary of Paderewski at the piano.

In short, you had better send this letter on to your principal, with my homages.

Yours faithfully,

G. Bernard Shaw.

10 Adelphi Terrace, W.C.

16th November, 1904.

Dear Golding Bright,

I promised to take 5% for what we should call No. 3 towns
—for places to which it was clearly not worth Daly's while to go.
But, of course, this does not mean that he can send a company
to Chicago and pay me 5% merely because he is not playing
himself. I should not, of course, object to his banging in a stray
No. 2 town to sweeten the bargain for the poor wretch to whom
he sublets his refuse ; but I should demur to any town of, say,
more than 100,000 population going in that way.

In short, I will take 5% in places where the piece evidently
would not be produced at all at the higher percentages.

Yours ever,

G. Bernard Shaw.

10 Adelphi Terrace, W.C.

22nd November, 1904.

I will fix up a meeting with Tyler this week if I can extricate
myself for a moment from rehearsals.

There will be a bit of fight on the S.S. committee over the
plays to be produced this season. With two such trump cards

as a new act, and Miss Ashwell, I shall have a try for second place (Tolstoy, *whom Redford has licensed,* has the first). Can you promise her ? I am curious to see the new act ; but that is only a matter of my personal literary appetite.

G. Bernard Shaw.

The Old House,   10 Adelphi Terrace, W.C.
    Harmer Green, Welwyn.
                                       8th March, 1905.

I cannot take "John Bull " out of Daly's hands and toss it to a stranger without a word of warning. Daly has done very well with my plays : why should I now wantonly throw him over and let the other fellows profit by his risk and his devotion ? Tell your man to go away and write a play for himself if he wants one.

I proposed to Tree to give a matinée for Viola of the first act of "Cæsar " : that is how he came to have the book, etc.

I do most seriously resent being bothered about productions. These idiots leave me in peace for ten years and then rush for me because the King orders a performance at the Court Theatre. They will make just as great a mess of producing me as they did before of *not* producing me. Put them off. Order them off. Call the police, if necessary. Daly and Vedrenne-Barker can still have me at 10% : all others 25%.

G. B. S.

The Old House,   10 Adelphi Terrace, W.C.
Harmer Green, Welwyn.

13th March, 1905.

I had to write to Frohman direct, as your revelation came the very day I had to ask him to lend me Ainley for "Man and Superman." However, he lent him and was very handsome about that and things in general. You might let me know when he returns to London. I had a satisfactory interview with Sam Shubert. Probably we shall pull off "Brassbound" after all with Miss Rehan.

I will send you the script you ask for presently. I want to take a final look through it so as to be able to say definitely what it wants in the way of trimming.

G. B. S.

10 Adelphi Terrace, W.C.

23rd February, 1906.

Dear Golding Bright,

What authors do you collect amateur fees for besides myself?

If your amateur business is at all large, or if it is worth your while to develop it, you should send a circular at least once a year to all the amateur dramatic clubs giving your list of authors and plays, terms, etc., etc. If it is not worth your while

to do this, I will send a circular on my own account ; and I may
as well include in it any other authors you are acting for.

Yours ever,

G. Bernard Shaw.

Plays, Pleasant
and
Unpleasant

1. Widowers' Houses
2. The Philanderer
3. Mrs. Warren's
        Profession
} Unpleasant Plays

4. Arms and The Man
5. Candida
6. The Man of Destiny
7. You Never Can Tell
} Pleasant Plays

Three Plays
for
Puritans

8. The Devil's Disciple
9. Cæsar and Cleopatra
10. Captain Brassbound's Conversion

11. The Admirable Bashville—
        Elizabethan parody
12. Man and Superman.

The above is a complete list of Mr. Shaw's plays up to date ;
but only Nos. 4, 5, 6, 7, 10 and 11 are suitable for amateurs of
ordinary aims and resources. Other lists should be given, of
course.

Amateurs desirous of performing plays by the above authors should apply to Miss Elizabeth Marbury, 20 Green Street, Leicester Square, London, W.C. (Registered Telegraphic Address: "Amarantes London"). The fee for single performances is £5.5.0 (or whatever it may be). For two performances, £8.8.0. Permission must be obtained beforehand, as certain plays by these authors are not always available for amateurs.

Applications are occasionally made for the remission of fees on the ground that the performance is for the benefit of a charity. Miss Marbury begs to point out that practically all amateur performances are for the benefit of charities ; so that an author who remitted fees on that ground would be not only giving a considerable part of his income in charity in addition to his direct personal contributions, but allowing amateur actors to choose the objects of his benevolence for him ; and this, too, without any guarantee that the business arrangement of the performance would be economical enough to leave any surplus for the charities. Such a request is obviously unreasonable. In no case can Miss Marbury remit the fees, or forward to the author any application for their remission.

All plays in Miss Marbury's hands are fully protected, and may not be performed without the author's authority in the United Kingdom.

Copies of Mr. Bernard Shaw's plays, at one-and-sixpence each, can be obtained from Miss Marbury. These are exact reprints of the original editions. The stage directions, though they contain no technical terms and seem to be of a purely literary character, contain all the information needed by the stage manager.

10 Adelphi Terrace, W.C.

11th May, 1906.

My plays have been purchased largely in Hungary by the theatres from various agents ; and " The Devil's Disciple " has been produced with great success.

The Authors' Society is now taking proceedings on my behalf, as the agents omitted to mention the matter to me or to send me any of the advances they collected in my name.

In short, the answer to your question as to how the plays stand in Hungary is—STOLEN.

G. B. S.

10 Adelphi Terrace, W.C.

The Flag of Boodle Pest.

You cannot persuade me.

If he paid hundreds, he owed millions.

G. B. S.

Address telegrams to   10 Adelphi Terrace,
" Socialist London."

London, W.C.

10th January, 1907.

Dear Golding Bright,

The question of "John Bull's Other Island " and the subsequent plays is settled for amateurs for the present by the fact
that none of them are as yet printed. When I have got them
through the press there is no reason why "John Bull " and
" Man and Superman " at least should not be played by amateurs
if they want to. " Major Barbara " is beyond them : you are
not likely to have any applications. " The Doctor's Dilemma "
will not be printed for some time yet.

French used to reduce the five-guinea fee to four guineas
when two performances were given ; but, on the whole, I think
I shall leave matters as they are. I have no sympathy at all with
amateurs on the money question, because any money they make
they give away to some hospital or other, and thereby encourage
the private charity system which I have been preaching against
all my life. The money goes first into the pocket of the rate-
payer, who is relieved from the duty of providing public
hospitals, and it is then screwed out of him by the landlord as
rent, the upshot of the whole transaction being that I lose two
guineas and you lose your commission on it for the sake of the
Duke of Westminster or the Duke of Bedford.

I am greatly flattered by Leslie Stuart's desire to collaborate
with me in a musical play. Ever since 1894 I have been overwhelmed with commissions of that sort, beginning with D'Oyly
Carte, who gave me *carte blanche* for a Savoy opera and told
me I need not have Sullivan unless I chose. Then came George
Edwardes, who selected me as the original librettist of " The

Duchess of Dantzic." Lowenstein and others followed, but that great libretto is still unwritten. Tell Stuart that I am rather keen on the idea, but that what I want to write is the music and not the libretto.

Yours ever,

G. Bernard Shaw.

R. Golding Bright, Esq.,
20 Green Street,
Leicester Square, W.C.

With Bernard Shaw's   10 Adelphi Terrace, W.C.
compliments.

14th February, 1907

By the way, five nights at Liverpool of " You Never Can Tell " is past a joke. If amateurs are going into business like this, they must pay business rates. We must confine amateurs to two performances at the outside ; for this affair amounts to a breach of my understanding with Vedrenne and Barker.

G. B. S.

G. Bernard Shaw, Esq.,
10 Adelphi Terrace,
Strand, W.C.

Dear Mr. Shaw,

In a cable just received from Australia we are asked to secure the Australian rights of " Mrs. Warren's Profession." Would you let me know if you will agree to negotiate for these rights and, if so, what would your lowest terms be, as we have to cable the reply as soon as possible.

With kindest regards,

Yours sincerely,

Ada Wooldridge.

15/2/07.   10 Adelphi Terrace, W.C.

Certainly not at present. It will not do to begin Australian operations with " Mrs. Warren's Profession." I prefer always to hold back that play until my position is firmly established with less controversial pieces.

G. B. S.

Ayot St. Lawrence, Welwyn, Herts.

Station : Wheathampstead, G.N.R., 2¼ miles.

Telegrams : Bernard Shaw, Codicote.

10 Adelphi Terrace, W.C.

27th February, 1907.

Dear Miss Wooldridge,

Seven performances mean simply seizing the Dublin rights under cover of amateurism. If the Players' Club choose to give seven private performances to their own members, they can have that luxury by paying for it ; but seven public perform-ances are quite out of the question ; and even to the private ones the press must not be invited.

Have we any particulars of where the performances are to take place, where the money is to go, etc., etc. ?

The Liverpool affair was bad enough ; but this would be an outrageous abuse of the right to license amateurs.

I return to town tomorrow.

In haste to catch the post,

Yours,

G. Bernard Shaw.

10 Adelphi Terrace, W.C.

3rd March, 1907.

Dear Golding Bright,

We must shut down on these Dublin people firmly. Write to them and ask them how they can possibly require the Gaiety Theatre in Dublin for a week if their performances are really amateur ones. Point out that you have no authority to deal with my plays in England except for amateur purposes, and that, in any case, they can hardly suppose that my plays can be performed by anyone who chooses to pay five guineas a night, at a regular theatre under commercial conditions. Say that if a club of amateurs choose to give seven performances at an occasional or private theatre for the amusement of their guests and themselves, that is their own affair, and they can get permission by paying for it ; but to take the second theatre in Dublin for a Shaw week, and present a play which has not been judged in that city by a professional performance, and claim amateur terms, is absurd.

If they choose to give their seven performances privately, without inviting the press, or selling tickets to the public for their own profit, or indeed selling to the public at all, then we might reluctantly permit it, as you overlooked the number seven in consenting. But if they mean business, they must make a business proposition, though there is no likelihood of their being allowed to anticipate Vedrenne and Barker.

They have done " The Man of Destiny " quite often enough. I shall not consent to their Shaw week, which is really a most impudent abuse of amateur business. The Liverpool affair was the last straw : I could have been sued for it if the aggrieved parties were any other than V. and B. ; and they are not particularly pleased, naturally.

113

After this, you must make a cast-iron rule never to permit more than two performances at the outside, and then only under genuine amateur conditions. You should be very chary indeed of giving permission for "Arms and the Man," "You Never Can Tell," and the "pleasant plays" generally in No. 1 towns where they have not been seen at the regular theatres. Otherwise you may get me into no end of trouble.

Yours faithfully,

G. Bernard Shaw.

10 Adelphi Terrace, W.C.

6th March, 1907.

Dear Golding Bright,

Will you please read the enclosed letter from me to Ashley ; make a copy of it to keep by you ; and post it today.

I enclose also Ashley's letter.

What has happened is that they made money out of "The Man of Destiny," and now want to make more out of "Arms and the Man." It is an awkward business ; and in future we must use a form of consent printed in strict terms. I shall not absolutely forbid the performances ; but they must pay 10% on the gross.

Do not take any further action yourself until I have Ashley's reply.

Yours faithfully,

G. Bernard Shaw.

IRISH PLAYERS' CLUB.   Innisfallen, Frankfort Avenue,

Rathgar, Dublin.

5th March, 1907.

Dear Sir,

I have to acknowledge receipt of your letter of the 4th inst. When we wrote you some time ago for permission to perform " The Man of Destiny " you referred us to your Agent, Miss Elizabeth Marbury, from whom, you said, we would get all information. Accordingly, when we desired permission to play "Arms and the Man " we wrote this Agent (whom, we presume, is invested with full powers regarding such matters) asking for permission to give seven consecutive performances—that is, a week including matinée—and what the fees would be. Your Agent replied giving permission as desired, naming fees, and accepting our cheque on account of such fees for these performances without placing any limitation or making any reservation whatever in regard to "Arms and the Man." We thereupon considered the matter arranged and accordingly concluded arrangements to present this play at the Gaiety Theatre for a week, as already stated, and in the event of our failure to carry out this contract we become liable to the extent of £300. You are, of course, bound by your Agent's contract with us and we have a perfect right, therefore, to give seven consecutive performances as stipulated for. However, with a view to meeting your wishes and in order not to involve you in any difficulty regarding your provincial rights (though we understand that this play has already been performed in Dublin), we got the theatre people to consent to alter the terms of the contract to four performances of "Arms and the Man " provided we filled up the other three performances with " The Man of Destiny." As we

115

consider this is a reasonable compromise in the circumstances, we hope you will place no further obstacles in the way of this arrangement, otherwise we shall have no alternative but to abide by our contract with the theatre.

Our reason for playing at the Gaiety is because there is no other place suitable or available, and, as a matter of fact, amateur companies usually perform at this theatre. We produced " Hedda Gabler " and " The Doll's House " at the Queen's Theatre, as well as " The Heather Field " (Edward Martyn) and " The Great Galcote " (Echegeray), playing for a week on each occasion, but this theatre is no longer available as it is now closed and coming down. So you will see that it is no unusual thing for us to play for a week. Indeed, we would never have thought of asking for permission to play "Arms and the Man " for a couple of nights, as it would be far too troublesome and expensive for such a short run.

We would further point out, in regard to what you say about first performances of your plays in the provinces, that we believe you gave permission to the Irish National Theatre Society to present "John Bull's Other Island " before a Dublin audience for the first time without any reservation whatever as to the number of performances, besides having already given us permission to play " The Man of Destiny " publicly for the first time here and without any reservation.

With regard to the *bona-fides* of our Club, I may mention that the Players' Club is one of the oldest amateur clubs in Ireland, well known and highly regarded. Mr. George Moore, your contemporary, was at one time our Stage Manager, and is still connected with us. You are not correct in assuming that we are inexperienced.

Now, we shall be glad to hear that you will end this unpleasant controversy over a business which has already been definitely concluded, and that you will agree to the compromise which we have been able to effect with the theatre, *i.e.* to play

"Arms and the Man" four nights and "The Man of Destiny" three nights, in order to carry out our engagement.

Awaiting your early reply,

I am,

Yours faithfully,

Anthony Evelyn Ashley,

Hon. Secretary.

George Bernard Shaw, Esq.

[COPY]

6th March, 1907.

Dear Sir,

The question at issue—which is of such importance to authors that I shall have to make a test case of it if you seriously claim that you can ask for permission to give an amateur performance and pay amateur fees, and then embark on a commercial theatrical speculation—is whether the week at the Gaiety Theatre is going to be a week of amateur theatricals or a week of ordinary theatrical business. What is the nature of your contract with the Gaiety? Are the terms sharing terms? And if there be a profit, where will that profit go to?

Until I am informed on these points I can say nothing more than I have already said. The principle involved is a most important one. It concerns a privilege which is worth, say, twenty guineas in the commercial market and five in the amateur market. To buy the privilege at amateur rates and then exploit it commercially, is a proceeding of which a very strong view indeed would be taken if it were attempted by a regular theatrical manager. I do not suggest that this aspect of the matter occurred to you ; but now that I put it plainly before you, you will, I think, see that I am not acting unreasonably. It is quite likely that the net profit on a week of "Arms and the Man " may at this moment reach and even considerably exceed £500 if you admit the public by payment at the doors and invite the press. You propose to obtain that profit by paying me a fee fixed on the assumption that there is to be no profit at all and that the enterprise is entirely disinterested as far as money is concerned. Naturally, I refuse to sanction this. If you are an amateur, you must confine yourself to amateur conditions. If you are a man of business, you must pay me business terms.

I hope I do not convey an impression of being unfriendly to your Club ; but you will see that it has sprung something on me which was never contemplated when the amateur conditions were fixed.

Yours faithfully,

G. Bernard Shaw.

A. Evelyn Ashley, Esq.,
Rathgar, Dublin.

10 Adelphi Terrace, W.C.

26th November, 1907.

I am told that the Garrick Society of Stockport played to over £100 with one of my plays at the Opera House, Buxton, and that they are arranging to give " three consecutive plays " in Liverpool as well as a performance in Oldham. If this is " amateur " business, then all amateur business must be stopped at once. The Liverpool affair is out of the question : it positively must not take place. Please authorise nothing—amateur or otherwise—in future without consulting me. I shall have actions for damages against me presently.

G. B. S.

Ayot St. Lawrence, Welwyn, Herts.

Station : Wheathampstead, G.N.R., $2\frac{1}{4}$ miles.

Telegrams : Bernard Shaw, Codicote.

27th November, 1907.

No : I haven't authorised anybody. My informant is the manager of the Manchester Playgoers' Theatre Co., who is touring with " Widowers' Houses."

Did the Stockport Garrick Society get leave for the alleged performance in Buxton ?

G. B. S.

Reply to Adelphi Terrace : I shall be up tomorrow (Thursday).

10 Adelphi Terrace, W.C.

3rd January, 1908.

As " You Never Can tell " has now been performed by the Vedrenne–Barker Co. in Manchester, there is no longer any reason for keeping it locked up in Manchester as far as single performances by amateurs are concerned. Still, be sure that the amateurs *are* amateurs. I write this because I see it stated in the *Manchester Evening News* that the West Didsbury Society (whatever that may be) got choked off Y.N.C.T.—possibly quite rightly ; but I thought I'd remind you that a tour had already passed through with Y.N.C.T. and "John Bull."

G. B. S.

Ayot St. Lawrence, Welwyn, Herts.

Station : Wheathampstead, G.N.R., $2\frac{1}{4}$ miles.

Telegrams : Bernard Shaw, Codicote.

2nd February, 1908.

Unless you hear from me to the contrary before Thursday, you can licence the Lincoln people for " Brassbound." The delay is to ascertain whether Ellen Terry is going there, in which case I should have to refuse.

The Surrey gentleman is all right. " How He Lied " and

" The Man of Destiny " count as one full-length play. Of course,
he must play at the place he mentioned, not elsewhere.

G. Bernard Shaw.

Miss Elizabeth Marbury,
20 Green Street,
Leicester Square, W.C.

Ayot St. Lawrence, Welwyn, Herts.

Station : Wheathampstead, G.N.R., $2\frac{1}{4}$ miles.

Telegrams : Bernard Shaw, Codicote.

The Woodford people may go ahead. If they wish me to
decide what is to be done with the profits (if any), I strongly
advised them either to keep them for the promotion of future
performances or give them to any public art gallery or the like
that may exist at Woodford. Failing that, let them get drunk
on it rather than give it to any charity.

G. Bernard Shaw.

Miss Wooldridge,
    Miss Elizabeth Marbury,   [Post-marked Oct. 30, 1908]
    20 Green Street,
    Leicester Square, W.C.

Ayot St. Lawrence, Welwyn, Herts.

Station : Wheathampstead, G.N.R., $2\frac{1}{4}$ miles.

Telegrams : Bernard Shaw, Codicote.

19th June, 1909.

" Major Barbara " is not available for amateurs yet.

G. B. S.

Miss Elizabeth Marbury,
20 Green Street,
Leicester Square, W.C.

Great Southern Hotel,

Parknasilla, Co. Kerry.

In answer to your letter of the 4th, these A.D.C.'s in Bolton, Liverpool, etc., can have the plays for *one* performance, but not for more. What must be stopped is the snatching of weeks in those towns under pretext of amateurism. In some cases I have found people actually announcing performances without leave under the impression that all they had to do was to send in £5.5.0 afterwards.

G. Bernard Shaw.

(Picture) Post Card
Miss Elizabeth Marbury,
20 Green Street,
Leicester Square, London, W.C.

Post-marked
Sept. 12, '09.
Co. Kerry.

Ayot St. Lawrence, Welwyn, Herts.

Station : Wheathampstead, G.N.R., 2¼ miles.

Telegrams : Bernard Shaw, Codicote.

10 Adelphi Terrace, W.C.

2nd November, 1909.

Dear Miss Wooldridge,

Whenever people ask for reductions or special privileges of any kind, tell them it is no use—that the fees and conditions of performances are not arranged by the author according to his fancy, but are determined by the whole body of authors acting through the Dramatic Committees of the Society of Authors, and that individual authors are not free to undersell one another by making reductions. The Vaudeville Dramatic Club and the Goldsmiths College (University of London), New Cross, must pay the usual fees.

The Green Room Amateur Dramatic Society of Liverpool may play two nights—Thursday and Saturday, NOT the charity night—*provided they do not select "Arms and the Man" or " Candida."* If they want either play, they can play it once only, as the two are on the road.

The Bolton A.D.C. can have the same reply—"Arms and the Man " once only.

Yours faithfully,

G. Bernard Shaw.

Address Telegrams to
" Socialist London."

10 Adelphi Terrace, W.C.

7th May, 1910.

Dear Golding Bright,

Before I say anything about " Major Barbara " I must ask Charles Frohman his intentions. He undertook to produce it ; but there was no contract. Still, it would be only civil to reopen the subject before I do anything decisive. Also " Major Barbara " is a play which requires a quite exceptionally strong company, including at least six first-rate people. Laurence Irving had better write to me direct about it. I doubt very much whether the play is within his resources.

Yours faithfully,

G. Bernard Shaw.

Address Telegrams to   10 Adelphi Terrace, W.C.
"Socialist London."

8th October, 1910.

Dear Miss Wooldridge,

In answer to your letter about Sutton and Surbiton, why do these people want to give three performances ? I think you had better always give a stereotyped reply to people who make requests of this sort, to the effect that a production for three nights is outside the usual scope of amateur enterprise, and that you can only submit the request to me with sufficiently full particulars to convince me that I am really dealing with amateurs and not with professionals, or semi-professionals, or local managers exploiting local amateurs commercially. It is absurd to waste our time in repeating the same correspondence again and again when the answer is always the same. Surbiton is a tolerably important suburb ; and if I were to make a contract for, say, Number 3 places with a little professional company, and they found that I have allowed them to be forestalled by these three-night ventures, they would have a very legitimate grievance against me. On the whole, we had better make it a fixed rule that three performances are only to be authorised under special circumstances and after very full information.

Yours faithfully,

G. Bernard Shaw.

Ayot St. Lawrence, Welwyn, Herts.

Station : Wheathampstead, G.N.R., 2¼ miles.

Telegrams : Bernard Shaw, Codicote.

18th February, 1913.

Dear Golding Bright,

You can let the amateurs loose on " Fanny's First Play " to their hearts' content. The only difficulty is that it is not yet published ; and as I can only lend a single copy, I don't see how performances can be managed until I get my new volume out.

The South African people have been at me about " Man and Superman." So have the Dutch people about " Fanny." They go to you in despair because I put off answering them for one reason or another. Don't bother about them. In the fullness of time I will attend to them personally.

Yours ever,

G. Bernard Shaw.

Address Telegrams to
" Socialist Westrand London."

10 Adelphi Terrace, W.C.

22nd October, 1913.

Dear Golding Bright,

" Pygmalion " is not really in the market at present, though I am, of course, always open to offers. What I mean by this is that though the rights are in my hands and subject to no contract affecting America, yet I have privately made up my mind as to what I am going to do with them. In any case, I could not quote general terms. You know roughly that I have often done business at a straight 10% for America and that this may be regarded as a minimum ; but a good deal depends on the manager with whom I am dealing. In any case, if the manager does not wish to deal with me directly and approaches me through you, it must be understood that you are acting as his agent and not as mine. As I shall have to do all the work, it is only fair that he should pay all the commission. Anyhow, *I* won't pay any.

I wish you would give up agency and take to honest industry. The older I grow, the more violently I find myself prejudiced against agents of all sorts.

Yours ever,

G. Bernard Shaw.

10 Adelphi Terrace, W.C.

19th December, 1914.

" The Dark Lady of the Sonnets " is for the present in Miss Gertrude Kingston's hands, who is now in New York arranging for its production with three other plays of mine.

G. Bernard Shaw.

Next week :   GRAND THEATRE, BIRMINGHAM.
Opera House, Southport.

4th January, 1916.

My dear Bernard Shaw,

How about your play " Flaherty, V.C." ?
I am starting management again at a theatre that I think might interest you. Would you like me to read it ; or would you rather see me in hell first ?

Yours, etc.,

Arthur Bourchier.

128

Ayot St. Lawrence, Welwyn, Herts.

6th January, 1916.

My dear Bourchier,

I am sorry to say that the war is an impossible subject for the theatre just now. I have written not only "O'F" but another little play about it, only to be driven to the conclusion that they would be unbearable. Even "Arms and the Man," dating from 1894, jars. It was played on New Year's Day in Scotland before—among others—a colonel home on leave from the front. He said it was quite extraordinary how I knew all about it without any experience, and that Loos was just like the charge at Slivnitza as I described it : " simple suicide : only the pistol *did* go off " (in the play it didn't) ; but for that very reason he could hardly stand it. The touch of our art makes the thing live ; and nobody could bear the war if it was real to them. Just think of the chance of a piece of bad news on the day of your first night ! Excuse my using your letter—war economy !

Ever,

G. Bernard Shaw.

129

E

10 Adelphi Terrace, W.C.

9th October, 1919.

Tell William Morris there is no use approaching me.

I have half-a-dozen solid proposals in figures in my desk made directly to myself ; and it is open to any man to add to their number if he feels that way. I am not likely to accept any of them ; but the shop is open, and all customers receive respectful attention.

Why not offer to take on the lectures yourself ? You could deliver quite a good set on the theatre, and on London celebrities.

G. Bernard Shaw.

10 Adelphi Terrace,

London, W.C.2.

17th October, 1925.

Dear Golding Bright,

Nobody but myself has any rights whatever in "Arms and the Man."

The history of " The Chocolate Soldier," as far as I was concerned in it, is this. I saw a press paragraph to the effect that Oscar Strauss was making a musical version of "Arms and the Man." I wrote to him warning him not to infringe my rights.

He did not reply ; but soon afterwards I received an appeal *ad misericordium* from Herr Jacobson not to ruin him by forbidding the performance of " The Chocolate Soldier," as he had written the libretto, of which he sent me a copy. I read it, and found that he had used certain scraps of my dialogue, the effect of which in the context of his stuff was so bad that I improved the piece considerably by cutting them all out. I then told him I would have nothing whatever to do with " The Chocolate Soldier " ; but if none of my dialogue was used I did not think I could appeal to the courts successfully to stop the performance, because (a) parodies and travesties of standard serious works are privileged by custom, (b) I had clearly no rights in the Servo-Bulgarian war as a dramatic subject, and (c) the incident of a fugitive soldier taking refuge in a lady's bedroom was too common to be patented by me or anyone else. There were no other features in " The Chocolate Soldier " apart from the title which could be found in "Arms and the Man." Jacobson's characters were all cads, cowards, vieux marcheurs, and prostitutes with names invented by himself. His libretto was not a play, but a putrid *opéra bouffe* in the worst taste of 1860. Under these circumstances I did not propose to take any steps provided my name was not connected with the thing in any way.

Even with this Herr Jacobson was not satisfied. He pleaded that he would be accused of plagiarism if he were not allowed to say that he had borrowed an incident from "Arms and the Man " ; and I said that he might say what he liked provided he conveyed no suggestion that I was in any way responsible for his libretto, or that Oscar Strauss's score was a setting of "Arms and the Man."

I never departed from this attitude. It was evident that they all believed that I could have stopped " The Chocolate Soldier," because they all offered to pay me a royalty. Mr. Whitney, who produced the play in America, was very anxious about me, as it seemed unaccountable that I should refuse money when there was so much of it going. But it was just because there was so much money in it that I did not stop it. It gave a lot of employment to the artists and others, and plenty of enjoyment to the public. Then there was Strauss to be considered. He was not to blame, as he evidently knew nothing about the copyright question. So I let them alone ; and they all flourished exceedingly.

I believe I told Miss Marbury to come down on them if they used any of my dialogue in the American version ; but as she was not collecting any fees for me she had no interest in the matter, and took no action. I afterwards found that some of my dialogue had been used.

Now that the film question has arisen over the success of the Theatre Guild production of "Arms and the Man," I shall probably deal with it just as I did with " The Chocolate Soldier." If they make a film of " The Chocolate Soldier " by Strauss, Jacobson & Co., I may not meddle with them. But if they bring my name into it, or connect it with "Arms and the Man " in any way, then I shall come down on them at once.

I cannot, however, answer for the attitude of the Theatre Guild. It may object to the release of a film called " The Chocolate Soldier " as an infringement of their interest in the play ; and they might possibly get an injunction.

In any case, Mr. Rumsey will not find it worth his while to interfere, as I will not be bought off by a royalty or anything of that sort, and there will, therefore, be nothing for him to collect. I shall instruct my American lawyer to warn Mr. Goldwin, and also put the Theatre Guild on its guard.

By the way, I shall have to take the amateur business out of the hands of Miss Marbury (that is, I suppose, out of the hands of the American Play Company) if I do not receive my fees regularly as I used to. My American Income Tax returns were

upset last time by a quite inexcusable delay. Perhaps they will
wake up if you jog them.

Faithfully,

G. Bernard Shaw.

Telegrams :   4 Whitehall Court,
" Socialist, Parl-London."

London, S.W.1.

19th January, 1928.

My dear G.B.,

In reply to yours of the 30th December asking, on behalf of
your New York office, whether I am prepared to negotiate for
the world film rights of "Arms and the Man," I am prepared to
negotiate with anybody about anything in the course of my
business, provided the anybody is a principal or the agent of a
principal, and is not proposing to negotiate as my agent. As
you may imagine, I do not need introductions to the film firms :
they come to me when they mean business. You had better tell
your New York people that there is nothing for them in it.

I have no objection on principle to being filmed ; but I have
to consider the effect on my ordinary theatrical business ; and
my general policy is to wait until I have had a revival which
shelves the play for five years or so before putting it on the
filmable list. Also, this Movietone development is complicating
the question a good deal.

Ever,

G. Bernard Shaw.

133

INDEX

136